UNHEARD VOICES
OF THE PANDEMIC

NARRATIVES FROM THE FIRST YEAR OF COVID-19

EDITED BY DAO X. TRAN

Transcribers
Willa Rae Culpepper, Brenna Miller, Paul Skenazy, Aileen Thong, Yuko Yokoi

Interviews and additional editing by
Ela Banerjee, Mateo Hoke, Marci Denesiuk, Virginia Eubanks,
Cliff Mayotte, Audrey Petty, Katrina Powell, Andrea Quijada,
Sara Sinclair, Gabriel Thompson, Dao X. Tran

Fact-Checking
Rebecca McCarthy

UNHEARD VOICES
OF THE PANDEMIC
NARRATIVES FROM THE FIRST YEAR OF COVID-19

EDITED BY DAO X. TRAN

Haymarket Books
Chicago, Illinois

**VOICE OF
WITNESS**

www.haymarketbooks.org
info@haymarketbooks.org

ISBN: 978-1-64259-713-4

Distributed to the trade in the US through Consortium Book Sales and Distribution (www.cbsd.com) and internationally through Ingram Publisher Services International (www.ingramcontent.com).

This book was published with the generous support of Lannan Foundation and Wallace Action Fund.

Illustrations by Gregory Ballenger, Jose Cruz, Hannah Lee, and Christine Shields.
Cover design and interior layout by Erik Freer, https://freer.studio
Cover image by Amber Bracken.

For all those who tell their stories against the greatest odds,
and for all those whose stories have been cut short during this pandemic

INTRODUCTION   1

ROBERTO VALDEZ, Thermal, California   4
"We are like chess pieces that politicians move around"

SHEAROD McFARLAND, Jackson, Michigan   10
"Cage on top of cage"

FARIDA FERNANDEZ, Los Angeles, California   16
"Underfunded, understaffed, underresourced"

HANIMA EUGENE, Oakland, California   22
"Formerly incarcerated people are struggling"

RAUL LUNA GONZALEZ, El Paso, Texas   28
"It was impossible for us to protect ourselves"

CLAUDINE KATETE, Roanoke, Virginia   36
"I'm the only one working"

SOLEDAD CASTILLO, San Francisco, California   42
"How are we going to pay these bills?"

BLAINE WILSON, Tsartlip First Nation   48
"I feel like it's the old days"

GABRIEL MÉNDEZ, San Francisco, California   54
"Even in a pandemic, we're still a minority"

MICHAEL "ZAH" DORROUGH, Corcoran Prison, California   60
"Fighting too hard and for too long to go out from a virus"

EMMANUEL RODRÍGUEZ, Mayagüez, Puerto Rico   66
"Getting money was such a relief"

NINA GONZALEZ, San Mateo, California **72**
"We're in survival mode right now"

HUNTER R., Albuquerque, New Mexico **78**
"Online sex work is not easy money"

ANASTASIA BRAVO, Bronx, New York **84**
"Millions of us contribute to this country without having any status here"

YUSUFU MOSELY, Chicago, Illinois **90**
"You feel a lot of anxiety coming from people"

MOHAMMED "MIKE" ALI, Bay Area **96**
"There's six of us living in a three bedroom"

OSCAR RAMOS, Salinas, California **102**
"Two of those missing students are from my class"

ACKNOWLEDGMENTS **108**

INTRODUCTION

In March 2020, COVID-19 was declared a pandemic, and we at Voice of Witness (VOW)— like many in the world — found our workplace, projects, and plans turned upside down. We dealt daily with uncertainty. At VOW, our work of amplifying unheard voices and centering the stories of historically marginalized and oppressed people and groups through oral history is deeply rooted in holding space for interviewees, whom we call narrators, and connecting through in-person listening. We asked ourselves: *How do we continue this vital work? Is oral history storytelling under these new conditions even possible?*

But the need to respond to the pandemic and its effects was clear. In the initial rush of media coverage, COVID-19 was characterized as a widespread crisis, altering life for all in the same ways: a "great equalizer." We knew, however, that the pandemic was disproportionately affecting our narrator communities, already among the most marginalized communities in the US.

At VOW, we pride ourselves on curating and crafting with our narrators and editors long-form, deeply felt, and meticulously edited and researched anthologies. Usually we work on these projects for years before publication. But the pandemic and the accompanying crises around unemployment, housing and food insecurity, and inadequate health care clearly called for something else—a more urgent, collective response.

We called on our narrators, editors, grassroots partners, and community

1

members to engage in a process with VOW to gather the stories of what was happening in our communities, to begin to uncover and learn together about the many ways that the pandemic was magnifying already existing inequities and acting as yet another vector for the spread of injustice. The response was tremendous. Narrators were eager to tell their stories, to be heard, to illuminate some of the hard truths about the pandemic. We listened and held space for them — through computer screens and emails, video chats and phone calls — their voices persisting even when WiFi and cell reception crackled.

The pieces included in this collection are from interviews conducted between April 2020 and March 2021. Stories came from across the mainland United States, as well as Puerto Rico and Canada. Shearod McFarland took us to Jackson, Michigan, where the virus was sweeping through prison cells. Farida Fernandez walked us around a COVID ward in Los Angeles. Anastasia Bravo, a housecleaner and a single mother, guided us around her neighborhood in the South Bronx. All were witnesses to how the pandemic was further deepening the injustices faced by their communities.

Roberto Valdez, an undocumented farmworker in California's Coachella Valley, was one of the narrators in VOW's book, *Chasing the Harvest: Migrant Workers in California Agriculture* (2017), and his was the first piece in the Unheard Voices of the Pandemic series to appear in the *Guardian*. We partnered with *Salon*, the *Nation*, and *Prism* to publish subsequent pieces.

This print collection is being released more than a year after the start of the pandemic, when over six hundred thousand people have died in the US from COVID-19 (a number that will undoubtedly continue to rise, in spite of effective vaccines). *Unheard Voices of the Pandemic* tells the stories of seventeen of the many individuals who have been impacted by the myriad and interlocking crises that preceded and were magnified by the pandemic.

We invite readers to a mutual sighting with our narrators, to experience the connection and sense of community that we felt as we worked on this collection. Working on this series helped us feel less isolated—and it was a chance to act, to amplify narrator voices in disrupting systems of injustice. In his narrative, when a box of groceries is left at his door anonymously, Roberto reflects: "It meant that someone was thinking about us, that someone was worrying about us. This was a gesture of kindness toward us." Although the shadow cast by the COVID-19 pandemic is long, we hope the insights gleaned through listening will last longer.

In solidarity,
Ela Banerjee, Community Partnership Coordinator
Rebecca McCarthy, Editorial Assistant
Annaick Miller, Communications and Outreach Manager
Dao X. Tran, Managing Editor

June 2021

ROBERTO VALDEZ

AGE: 52
LOCATION: Thermal, California

For more than two decades, Roberto Valdez has harvested crops in California's Eastern Coachella Valley, a scorching region dotted with impoverished communities that are surrounded by bountiful fields of grapes, bell peppers, broccoli, watermelon, and more. In 2005, after his son nearly died from heat stroke while picking grapes, Valdez advocated for improved safety measures for farmworkers, which culminated in new state regulations that protect workers from heat stress. An undocumented immigrant, he is not eligible for federal relief during the COVID-19 pandemic, but while millions of people shelter in place, he continues to work in the fields with his wife, Leticia.

Right now I'm harvesting eggplant for $13 an hour. The company gives the crew a $0.50 bonus for each box we fill, so in eight hours we can earn an extra $15 or so, in additional to our wages. The plants are about four feet tall and the eggplants grow low, so we usually work on our knees in the dirt. You cut off the eggplants with scissors and fill up buckets that weigh between forty and fifty pounds, carry them to a large tub where they are washed and packed, and dump them in.

It tires you out, especially when it's hot. It was 105 degrees today. By ten o'clock in the morning your clothes are completely soaked with sweat and it's hard to make it through the eight hours. In fact, some days there are people who leave, who can't make it.

Because of the coronavirus we always cover our faces now, no matter what the temperature is. The company has given us disposable blue masks, but we mostly use bandanas. The masks don't stay clean for very long and they start to smell. When they're dirty, it's very hard to breathe. The sun is hot, the ground is hot, you're working fast, and you can't breathe. A bandana you can wash and use again. I bring three bandanas every day: one that goes over my head to protect my neck, and two that I use as masks. We have breaks every four hours, and I use that time to wash the old one out with water and soap and put on a new one. My wife and I work together on the crew, and I bought sixteen bandanas that we use.

We leave two rows between each person now, a distance of about eight feet. Before, we ate lunch together around portable tables in the shade. We'd share food. "Hey, grab a taco!" That's all over. Now we eat apart, mostly in our cars. I also can't greet people like I used to do, either. I'm the kind of person who likes to shake hands, pat people on the back. "How's it going? How're you doing this morning?" Among us Latinos, that's very common. That's over, too.

But we still joke and talk, even though we're separated. There are about thirty people in the crew, and some of us have worked together for years. There are people who are tired, and we'll tell them a story, just so they'll be able to get through the day—that's how we make the work more bearable. Some people have had to stop working because of the coronavirus. There's a young woman, a single mother with two kids, and she couldn't keep working because the schools and daycares have shut down. It's very hard right now—so many mothers have had to stay home.

You have to respect this disease. My brother-in-law died eight days ago, in Mexicali. He was in his forties and worked at a plant that makes glass. He had high blood pressure and kidney problems, and they had to operate on his kidneys in March. While he was in the hospital he had a hard time breathing, and they suspected he had the coronavirus. They isolated him and put him in an area where the COVID-19 patients were. They didn't give my sister any information about how he was doing. The government said he died of the coronavirus, but we're still waiting for the official cause of death. It hurt us a lot, because he was a very good person and no one could visit him.

Yes, you have to respect this disease. I saw a news report from New York, where doctors were saying that people weren't keeping quarantine—going out even when they were supposed to be at home, and more people got infected. That's something we think a lot about. We stay very clean at work, because we know innocent people are buying the food we harvest, with money they have earned, so that their families will be healthy. And the majority of farmworkers, we're happy to work, we do so with love, and the coronavirus won't stop us. It's not going to stop us. Because we know that our work supports the whole nation.

Right now Governor Gavin Newsom has proposed giving undocumented immigrants $500 each. There are people who have sued to try and stop this, a woman named Jessica Martinez and a man from El Salvador, Ricardo Benitez.[1] I'd like these people to come out and meet us. I'd like them to see us working. There are people out here who really need this $500, especially people who have lost their jobs. We are the people who are feeding the country. No one else is going to be able to do this. We are the only ones who know how.

We are people who've lived in the country ten and twenty years, and we don't have a social security number. From my point of view—I say this from my heart—we are like chess pieces that politicians move around. They haven't done anything, since Barack Obama, since Bill Clinton, since 9/11. I remember I was picking grapes in Arvin when they attacked the Twin Towers.[2] Back then there was talk of immigration reform for workers. I had hope that it would happen. So we've had hope for a long time, and nothing has happened. We pay taxes. We go to stores and we buy things. Our kids are studying in school. My daughter is about to graduate high school. It's hard for me to understand why they aren't letting us become legal residents.

In the media, they're now calling us "essential workers." But that's what we've

1. In April, a nonprofit, the Center for American Liberty, filed an emergency petition with the California Supreme Court seeking to block California governor Gavin Newsom from allocating $75 million to help undocumented immigrants, who don't qualify for unemployment insurance. The plaintiffs in the lawsuit are Jessica Martinez, a councilwoman in Whittier, and Ricardo Benitez, an immigrant from El Salvador who is now a US citizen.
2. Arvin, a city of 22,000 people in the Central Valley, is located 15 miles southeast of Bakersfield and is a major producer of grapes.

always been. We think of doctors, firefighters, and police as important. People who never saw us before now see that we also have value. Look, I feel like this: the coronavirus has brought us both good and bad opportunities. It has hurt us, and it has also made many people realize something they didn't realize before: that they need us.

Last Monday I arrived home from work and there was a box at my door. The box was filled with milk, bags of lettuce, cabbage, onions, and potatoes. I don't know who brought us the food. I asked the person who manages the trailer park, and he just said some people came to drop off food for everyone. It made me want to cry. It meant that someone was thinking about us, that someone was worrying about us. This was a gesture of kindness toward us. Nothing like that had happened before.

Note: Roberto's name was changed to protect his privacy.

Interview and editing by Gabriel Thompson. Roberto is a narrator in and Gabriel is the editor of the Voice of Witness book Chasing the Harvest: Migrant Workers in California Agriculture. *This piece was published in the* Guardian *on May 28, 2020.*

SHEAROD McFARLAND

AGE: 52
LOCATION: Jackson, Michigan

Shearod McFarland was born and raised in Detroit. As a teenager, he was convicted of second-degree murder and a felony firearms charge and sentenced to twenty-five to forty years in Michigan state prisons. Shearod has spent more than thirty years behind bars, with more than eleven of those years in solitary confinement.

Of the top fifty COVID-19 clusters in the United States, thirty-three are prisons or jails. With COVID-19 wreaking havoc in detention facilities throughout the United States, at the time of this writing in May 2020, Michigan ranked second in the number of confirmed cases in state prisons and had the highest prison death toll of any state. Shearod communicated with us via the prison email system to describe what is currently happening at Parnall.

I'm incarcerated in Parnall Correctional Facility in Jackson, Michigan, where COVID-19 is sweeping through. My life and the lives of hundreds of other incarcerated men have changed dramatically since this pandemic began.

I started taking COVID-19 seriously when it really began spreading in New York. My fiancée lives in the Bronx, and the first cluster of cases in the state were in Westchester County, which is right outside the Bronx. I was fixated with the thought of her contracting the virus and had to fight off the sense of dread that I felt. Loss has been a constant in my life so it's always lurking in the back of my mind. I didn't want to experience another serious loss to this strange virus.

I heard about the first two confirmed cases of coronavirus at Parnall back in early March. Within weeks those two initial cases quickly turned into hundreds of infections. So far, Michigan prisons have over fourteen hundred confirmed cases and more than fifty prisoner deaths. Parnall has had ten of those deaths, and counting.

It's very difficult to get an accurate picture of just how many men here have been infected because at the beginning of the crisis the department's response to the sick was to quarantine them in empty cells by themselves. What kind of option is that? You get sick and basically have to be placed in solitary? Not an attractive prospect. So, unfortunately, many of the men decided that unless they became dangerously ill they would deal with the virus on their own, rather than seek medical help. The official number of infected here at Parnall is less than two hundred, but in reality the numbers are way higher than that. Maybe three to four times that figure.

This facility is nearly a hundred years old. It's a petri dish-like atmosphere, viruses spread incredibly fast. Two of the housing units here are built like a massive vertical zoo, just cage on top of cage. The other three units are open-air dorms that house nearly four hundred prisoners each, in what is probably less space than a small warehouse. Prisoners sleep, eat, shower, and use the bathroom in these human warehouses. So social distancing is virtually impossible.

We live in eight-man cubicles, which are approximately 20 x 13 feet. Each dorm has two communal showers, ten toilets, ten urinals, and eighteen sinks for every 192 men. There is also one "quiet room" and one TV room, which are both just a little bigger than the cubicles. So the spread of a highly contagious disease like COVID-19 is inevitable if it gets into the prison.

Living under such conditions is already a high-stress situation (which probably negatively affects your immune system), but having to face the threat of a deadly pandemic ups the ante by ten. I'm not ashamed to say that the fear of death by coronavirus has crossed my mind many times. I'm in my fifties, I have asthma, and I've been in prison nearly thirty-three years straight—making me one of the more "at risk." Some of the other men here are also quite vocal regarding their fears of the virus. But what can we do?

I personally know some of the men who have died from COVID-19. One was Garrison, who had been in prison for forty-four years, since he was sixteen years old. He was also just a few months from finally going home. After I heard about his death I felt horrible! I had to grieve for the man. To know that he'd spent over four decades in prison—from childhood to adulthood—only to die from this virus right when he was about to be released. It seems so tragic and unfair.

Parnall is a level-one (minimum security) facility, which generally means that the roughly two thousand men housed here get a lot of time for educational programming and recreation. But COVID-19 somehow entered the prison and changed all that. Now Parnall is like a segregated and abandoned ghost town.

Usually there's a lot of interaction here among the prisoner population. Social interaction is a huge part of prison life. It's how we break the monotony of incarceration. We study together, work out together, have spirited conversations, play basketball, cards, and board games like chess and checkers. But Parnall quickly became one of the epicenters of the outbreak in the Michigan Department of Corrections, and since then, all activities have ceased.

So on top of the typical soul-numbing boredom, the coronavirus has stripped us down to having even less to do. Currently, Michigan prisons have no main recreation yard or extracurricular activities like gym or weight pit. There are no visits, no educational programs running, no religious services, and no table games of any kind. All of these measures are understandable but difficult nonetheless.

Now a typical day for me has been mostly staying inside reading, talking on the telephone, and watching television. I'm an outdoorsy type, but in an attempt to control the spread of the virus within the population, the institution has separated the housing units and shut down the main recreation yard.

I'm someone who takes my mental and physical health very seriously. But now, being confined to an even smaller space than usual, I've found it impossible to get into a regular workout routine. I mean, I've been doing pushups, sit-ups, pullups, and the like, but it's hard. And ironic too. Because now since there is no main yard, a much larger group of men are forced into a much smaller area. Which means a crowd of people all trying to work out at once indoors. Annoying. Working out is my main way of relieving stress, and being so sedentary is having an effect on me. I'm eating more and gaining weight. Ugh! I hate it.

Also, wearing these face masks has become an issue. The department gave us the masks probably a month too late and now they're becoming a point of contention between prisoners and some officers. It's something else to harass us about. I mean, yes, I understand the necessity, but some staff are forcing us to wear them even when we're sitting all alone, with nobody within ten feet of us, or when we're working out.

I don't think that the state government has given the crisis in the prison system anywhere near what decency would require, but I can say that regardless of the value that society puts on our lives, we have been sources of support and assistance to each other. And that in itself is evidence of the rich human potential that lies behind the walls of prisons all over America.

Interview and editing by Mateo Hoke. Shearod is a narrator in and Mateo is a coeditor of the Voice of Witness book Six by Ten: Stories from Solitary. *This piece was published in* Salon *on July 11, 2020.*

FARIDA FERNANDEZ

AGE: 43
LOCATION: Los Angeles, California

Nurses are widely praised as selfless heroes of the coronavirus pandemic. But they face workplace and political conditions that routinely put them at unnecessary risk, hamper their ability to care for their patients, and discount their humanity and labor. Farida Fernandez, who asked to be identified by a pseudonym for fear of retaliation, is a nurse and community organizer from Los Angeles who is "willing to do anything right now for freedom," in both street protests and hospital halls.

I am a registered nurse and a community organizer working against state violence with the Stop LAPD Spying Coalition, centered in the community of Skid Row in Los Angeles. I am a daughter, a friend, and an intersex person.

I was born in Bellflower, California. When I was nineteen, I was summarily dismissed from my home—a lot of it having to do with my own mischievousness. Since then, I've lived in multiple communities in LA but have been settled in Long Beach for about six years.

I work in a hospital where 90 to 95 percent of the community members I serve are Latino, Latina, Latinx folk. They predominantly speak Spanish and have a lot of health conditions: diabetes, hypertension, and a lack of support. So, very sick people in the hospital—people working two to three jobs, a lot of undocumented folks who don't have insurance, people who have just never seen a doctor before.

I'm a medical-surgical nurse in an acute care unit. I'm also an oncology nurse. I treat a lot of lymphomas and leukemias, the kinds of cancer that people need to be hospitalized for about a week while they receive treatment.

I remember the last time I was in a gathering with lots of people—January 27—that date just rings in my ear, in my head. Someone asked me, "What do you think about this coronavirus?" Because I tend to live on the impending doom side, I was like, "Well, it could be really bad." But then I thought, *Maybe I'm being dramatic.* So I started to watch the LA County COVID counter, a Department of

Public Health website that tracks coronavirus infections and deaths. I remember when we were at twenty and we've now surpassed 275,000 cases.

By mid-February, I knew that this was going to be a problem. From March 3 to 5, my friend had a fiftieth birthday celebration, and we all went to Minnesota. I was really scared to go. The following Thursday, the pandemic was declared. I remember hugging a friend and almost crying. I thought, *This is the last time I'm ever going to hug somebody*. I still remember that last embrace. I don't think I've hugged anybody since.

Before my hospital had strict coronavirus isolation policies in place, in April 2020, I was exposed to a COVID-positive patient. I was the lead nurse that day and I had to assist another nurse in a bloody ninety-minute procedure. This patient had HIV, so I had gowned up with double gloves and I wore a face shield.

The following day, I was about to go out for a walk when I got a call from the hospital. They told me I had been exposed to a patient who was positive for COVID. But they told me I could still work as long as I wasn't symptomatic.

I was shocked. The CDC was advising that once you're exposed, you're supposed to quarantine for fourteen days. I had this moment of feeling really abandoned, struggling with figuring out the right thing to do. I immediately felt that I was going to be alone in it. That's the biggest, scary part of this virus: the isolation of being sick and being alone.

I remember another nurse telling me, "Just take leave. Maybe you can come back whenever." I was like, "What? Are you going to kick me out now? Because this calling to be a nurse, it's really true. I want to be there." I was confused, upset, emotional. I didn't know what to do.

At that point tests weren't readily available. I took a day off, using my sick leave, engaged all my organizer friends, and finally found a clinic. I drove an hour and a half. I begged them to test me. They said, "Fine, but don't tell your friends because we won't test them."

Then other organizer friends found an ear, nose, and throat doctor *at my hospital* who said, "We'll test you, don't worry. Give our number to every nurse at the hospital." I gave the number to my manager and to everybody else who was exposed. Everybody was able to get tested.

I went to my organizing community for help because I understood that this was a political problem. The FDA, the CDC, other countries were trying to give us access to testing. But with Trump, the United States was refusing help, deciding to make its own tests. This ultimately put us far behind in being able to isolate or quarantine people. People should still get tested, but contact tracing, isolation, and quarantine essentially only work at the beginning of an outbreak. We're beyond that now.

In the beginning of COVID, it was really chaotic; we didn't have tight systems in place. We were penalized for wearing masks—and nurses were showing up with N95s and face shields. We were very limited on what PPE we could have; we had to prove we needed them. And we are an oncology unit—we have to protect our patients who have weakened or no immune systems!

Now, we COVID screen every patient who is admitted to the hospital. But for several months, it felt like there were no procedures in place to protect us. I think my initial experience changed the policy.

At the end of June, though, I found out I had been exposed twice since then. Some of my patients had originally tested negative but started to have symptoms of COVID—fever, cough, fast heart rates, et cetera—and we decided to retest them. They had "converted"—now they tested positive. I was also asked to be part of a COVID unit, and I worked there for six weeks. Whether you are on a COVID or non-COVID unit, the danger of being exposed is everywhere.

Working in a hospital like mine, time and time again, you realize that you are underfunded, understaffed, underresourced. You realize that issues of health and wellness are not well understood—that social and political conditions create poverty and illness. This is what propelled me to become an organizer. I started to see how state violence maintains conditions of ill health.

For example, during COVID, Los Angeles has completely abandoned the community of Skid Row. There's no food, housing, or even clean water to wash one's hands. In response, organizations like Los Angeles Community Action Network have created mutual aid programs that not only provide healthy food but also build handwashing facilities throughout the community. The city has given up, but we have not!

I've been involved in the protests and uprisings around police brutality in Los Angeles, and I'm not the only one. Some doctors and managers at my hospital have shown up, which is great. It makes me feel not alone, makes me feel proud. I've been really happy to see on every flyer, "Mask up!" But I've also seen these rallies with people just standing there and shouting. I'm like, "Just march! Please start moving! Move through the air, open it up, take the streets. Just spread out, spread out."

People are willing to risk their lives, not just against the police and getting shot with rubber bullets and getting tear-gassed and hit with batons. They're willing to risk their health. It's like, "I may get a virus that may kill me." And that is amazing because against all odds, we are putting ourselves out there. The momentum is so strong right now. We're willing to do anything right now for freedom.

In the context of COVID and uprising, we need to embrace that this rebellion is really about structural racism. It's about how the Black community has been disenfranchised—from health care, housing, schools, land—and then controlled, contained, and criminalized by the police. We're not going to get out of this pandemic alive and preserve the lives of Black people unless those things are addressed.

That's why Black people are disproportionately dying of COVID: because everything you hear is about "COVID positive, COVID negative." None of it is about the structural issues that cause hypertension, diabetes, heart failure—all these things that make you *susceptible* to dying of COVID. Structural racism is killing Black people alongside the police.

In the beginning of the pandemic, I was seeing nurses drop like flies—go on leave, lose weight. Now, we're readjusting. I miss being able to hug my fellow nurse friends, because we need that camaraderie. I miss not being afraid to touch the patient, a kind of closeness that you could have without fear.

The job's already hard. It was already a crisis; it was already back-breaking. It was already a job that made you cry. But I cherish how strong everybody is.

Note: Farida's name was changed to protect her privacy.

Interview and editing by Virginia Eubanks. Virginia is a coeditor of the Voice of Witness project in incubation Living in the Digital Welfare State. This piece was published in Prism *on January 14, 2021.*

Illustration by Hannah Lee

HANIMA EUGENE

AGE: 42
LOCATION: Oakland, California

Hanima Eugene is a graduating college senior at UC Berkeley and a coordinator for the Underground Scholars Initiative, a student organization on the Berkeley campus that focuses on recruitment, retention, and advocacy for formerly incarcerated and system- impacted individuals.

I'm sitting at my desk. I'm looking at my computer screen and my cat, Isis, is sitting over to my right on her little pillow. And there are some plants. It's sunny, there are trees outside. It's airy and bright. My husband is normally here, but he's at work. He does construction, and all that work is continuing right now.

I'm born and raised in Oakland, California. And when I was younger, I went to schools in East Oakland. During the summertime they had a math, engineering, and science program, which was held at UC Berkeley. I remember going to that campus and I always said, "Hey, when I get older, this is the college that I want to go to." However, circumstances in my life led me to a violent domestic relationship and ultimately into prison for a term of fifteen years to life. During that time I put my focus back on my education.

I earned my associate's degree through a community college that offers courses to a number of California state prisons. One of the professors, Dr. Joan Parkin, basically challenged me and a friend. She said, "It's Berkeley or bust." And we were looking at her and looking at each other like, "What is she talking about?" She knew that incarcerated students were going to school at UC Berkeley. We couldn't believe it. She said, "You could also have the opportunity to go to Berkeley if you get good grades." She gave us a road map on what classes we needed to take, what we needed to do in order to get there. Three years later, I was up for parole.

And I made sure that I did all those things. So when I was released from prison in 2017, I immediately submitted my application to UC Berkeley and I was accepted.

I was sick on March 2, and there was notification that there was community spread in Solano County. I realized that COVID-19 was real. I don't get flu shots, and I normally don't suffer from the flu every year. But when I became sick for about seven days, I had all the symptoms. I had fever. I couldn't keep anything down for two days. I had chills and night sweats. I had a headache. I called Kaiser Health around day four and explained my symptoms. And the doctor was like, "It's just the flu." But I'm watching the news and I'm seeing all of this unfold. I also knew doctors didn't have tests and there was really nothing they could do. They told me, "Just stay home for two weeks. If it doesn't get better, contact us again." After that, there were signs of more people having infections or symptoms.

I'm a caregiver for my grandfather, who's eighty-eight years old. I don't know if I had COVID-19 or not, but I'm mindful of my grandfather and other vulnerable people who are more susceptible. My grandfather has ADT security monitoring for his house. He lives about ten minutes away from me. Since the shelter-in-place orders, I use that to log in and make sure to see him. He sits in the same chair every day. So I can see, hey, he's up and moving around. Or my husband and I go over there. We don't enter his home but talk to him through the screen door, with our masks on. And he sits at the door and we talk. Just to check in and see if he needs anything: groceries, food, stamps, because he mails a lot of his bills. You know, making sure he's okay. Before all this, he was already kind of isolated. A few of his friends would normally come by and visit, but they can't do that anymore. So I know it's extremely hard for him right now. And making sure that he doesn't feel alone or he has somebody to talk to is important to me.

I do miss my peers at school and advocates that I work alongside. I miss creating and strategizing with them. USI is the Underground Scholars Initiative, a student-run organization on the UC Berkeley campus that promotes educational opportunities and success for formerly and currently incarcerated students.

Imprisonment is glamorized in the US. All the TV, reality shows, music, provide a false narrative of what it means to be incarcerated. This is reflected during this pandemic when people on the news are talking about "lockdowns," "get out of jail free cards," "isolation," and "enforcement." This type of language forces me to reflect on the way society has interpreted the very harsh realities of prison life.

USI has been a bedrock for me these last two years. I feel like people understand me because a lot of times sitting in the classroom, I'm looking around for other faces that look like me and there aren't a lot. But being a member of USI dispels that feeling of being alone and lets me know, "Hey, I'm also supposed to be here on this campus."

Because this is my last year, my senior year, we would've been planning for graduation. This has been my best semester there. I was able to be on campus and network and really absorb what I've been learning without having to juggle a full-time job in addition to a full-time course load, and then this hit. It threw me for a loop mentally.

I fear our economy is going to be a lot worse off. I'm thinking about people like me who are graduating this year and what the employment field will look like after this. I have a feeling it's going to be really competitive. A lot of people are going to be looking for jobs, and I just have a lot of worry.

Before coronavirus, my typical day varied throughout the week. I had classes in the morning on campus. Then, from 1 to 2 p.m. I'd have another meeting. From 2 p.m. to 3:30 p.m., I go to the USI office, see if there are any letters from students who are incarcerated and need assistance. I help them with transcript analysis and data. And then, I have another class. After five o'clock, I'm normally off campus and headed home. I start preparing dinner, getting laundry done, getting ready for the next day. Sometimes I'm participating on coalition calls up until at least eight. And then off to bed. Then I wake up and do it all over again.

Now with COVID-19 and shelter in place, nothing is typical. I get restless. I've lost motivation. The university grading system defaulted to a pass/no pass model. So basically it's extremely hard for a person to not pass a course right now. You have to really be trying to not pass and that makes it easier for students to relax their studying habits. I'm like, this is my last year, I need to absorb everything that I can. So I'm trying to remain motivated when others around me are like, "Screw it," you know?

Yesterday I went out and purchased some plants and began rearranging, decorating, and cleaning my home. Putting some love into it. My plan is to work with incarcerated women, doing research on law and social factors, especially California murder and domestic violence laws that remain on the books and denote women as property. There are a lot of criminalized survivors in prison, so I want to collaborate with those women to perform research to create reports and develop some policy recommendations to support and help free them. My main concern is what the country will look like in the next couple months. I thought I had everything planned out. I was going to graduate; I had interviews scheduled. I thought I had it pretty mapped out so I could transition back into full-time employment. But coronavirus disrupted everything in my life.

We're in a moment where, you know, everybody needs help in some way. And how do we, with so many people needing help, prioritize? Folks can help by not forgetting that formerly incarcerated people are struggling and also have additional barriers.

During my incarceration, I found that people often forget, or fail to prioritize, people or things that are not part of their daily interactions. Therefore, speaking these "invisible" communities and people into spaces is a way of prioritizing them.

Note: Hanima's name was changed to protect her privacy.

Interview by Cliff Mayotte (education director at Voice of Witness) and Ela Banerjee (community partnership coordinator at Voice of Witness). Additional editing by Ela. This piece was published in Salon *on August 1, 2020.*

RAUL LUNA GONZALEZ

AGE: 39

LOCATION: El Paso, Texas

The coronavirus pandemic has been especially devastating for those behind bars, including immigrants held by Immigration and Customs Enforcement (ICE) who are locked up while their cases proceed. Medical care in these facilities is often substandard, and the tight quarters makes socially distancing impossible. Last year, Raul Luna Gonzalez, an immunocompromised asylum-seeker from Mexico, was transferred to a notorious immigration jail in Louisiana run by LaSalle Corrections, a for-profit corporation. Inside, as more people contracted the disease, ICE continued to deny Gonzalez's parole requests until he, too, became infected. Over several conversations, frequently interrupted by coughing fits, he spoke of why he fled Mexico and what he found when he arrived in the United States.

I arrived at the Richwood Correctional Center on June 13, 2019. My group was mostly Cubans—we had been moved from Texas to Mississippi to Louisiana. We were excited because we expected to be released soon. But at Richwood, the detainees told us that they don't give anyone parole or bond in Louisiana. They had a name for Richwood: the graveyard of living men. I asked to be released on parole anyway, but ICE denied me. They denied me many times.

I came to the United States because, until recently, I believed this was a country where you could find justice. Some people at Richwood thought I was crazy to carry all my files and audio recordings of the threats from the cartels. "But you have to prove what happened to you," I'd tell them.

I was a butcher in Acapulco, Mexico. In Acapulco, if you want to have a business, you have to pay a fee to the cartels, even if you're only selling lollipops. The Jalisco Nueva Generación cartel kept increasing the fee because they saw my business was doing well. I had nice cars and a house, and I went to fancy restaurants. I had eleven employees and gave them bonuses.

My employees took care of me, too. In 2014, I was diagnosed with colon cancer. When I got sick, they ran the shop. I endured twenty-eight radiation therapies, eight chemotherapies, and dropped to 104 pounds. There was a moment when I asked God to end my life. But my doctor told me something that I've guarded as a beautiful treasure: "Your mind is powerful. If you think you are going to live, and you fight to live, you will make it." In 2017, they took out forty-three centimeters of my intestine and rectum and installed a colostomy bag. I was back at work three months later.

By 2018, the cartel had raised the fee to a thousand pesos a week.[1] One Sunday, they took me to their boss. He proposed that I work for the cartel to identify wealthy people they could kidnap for ransom. I told him that I only wanted to run my business. Before I left he said, "Think carefully about it."

I kept paying the fee, but I refused to help the cartel. On February 18, 2019, I was at my friend's mechanic shop when an SUV pulled up and five men got out; two of them were the ones who collected the fee. They pulled me into the truck. One put a gun to my head. They drove me to a hill and forced me to walk into a forest. That's where I spent three days, with my hands and legs wrapped in duct tape. They hit and kicked me; one man urinated on me. They wanted 300,000 pesos, so I told them to call my mother. They told her, "Look, *señora*, we need this money now."

My family contacted the government and started working with an anti-kidnapping squad. I didn't know this at the time. I told the cartel they could take the cash I had in my house, my cars, and my gold jewelry. On February 20, the cartel told my sister to put the money and jewelry in a bag in my Jeep Patriot, park it at a certain spot, and leave the key under the driver's seat. They watched her park the car from the hill. But they were still going to cut me up with machetes.

---

1. A thousand pesos is roughly $45 US.

"You see, in this life there are no family or friends," the boss told me over the phone. "Now we have to kill you." I begged him to have mercy. I told him lies: that I'd give him 15,000 pesos a month and work for the cartel. I finally convinced him. My kidnappers couldn't believe it. One said, "Many people have come up here. You're the first who is going to leave this hill walking."

When I got home, I called my sister. I knew I needed to get out of there with my family. Minutes later, she arrived with the police, who said they had stopped my Jeep and arrested three men. I totally panicked. In Mexico, the police can't protect you from the cartels, and now the cartel would know my family went to the government. I thought for a long time and decided to negotiate. I'd tell the police everything I'd learned, but I needed a copy of the case file for proof of what had happened.

We hid at my brother Placido's house—he lived outside of Acapulco—and I shared what I knew. Meanwhile, the boss kept calling my sister, threatening us. As soon as we got the files, we drove to Juarez, where I have another brother. On the day we arrived, the boss called my sister. "Tell Raul that if he knows how to run, he should run as fast as he can. There's no place we can't find him, and when we do, I am going to personally cut him into pieces."

I crossed the bridge into El Paso on April 2, 2019. My sister, mother, and brother Placido crossed later, in Arizona. I introduced myself to an immigration officer. "I've come to ask for asylum. Here is my evidence." I thought I would live with my niece in El Paso, but instead they locked me up while I waited for my asylum hearing.

At Richwood I lived in a dormitory with more than a hundred men. They don't give you fruits or vegetables—it's always beans and rice. Sometimes we went twenty days without going outside. A lot of the guards were racist. When we'd go to the cafeteria, they'd say, "The pigs are coming for their rice." If we asked for something, they'd say, "Get out of here, wetback!"

These detention centers are designed to psychologically force people to give up. One of my friends was a Cuban named Roylan. He was a very positive person, very optimistic. He'd say, "Mexican, don't give up!" I'd yell back, "I won't!" He hung himself in his cell in October.

I cleaned my colostomy bag in the shower, where the walls are covered in mold and bacteria. In December, an infection made my genitals so swollen that I couldn't walk. My companions yelled for help, and the guards took me away in a wheelchair. The whole time, I was in handcuffs and chains were wrapped around my legs and waist. I asked, "Are you really going to lock me up? I can't even walk."

My asylum hearing was on March 27, 2020. The judge was on a video screen from New York; my attorney sat next to me. My sister and mother had already won asylum in Arizona, and I was sure I'd win mine, too, since I was the one who was kidnapped. I started to talk, but the judge interrupted. She said it wasn't necessary because she had already read the file. She said that she believed my story, but that she didn't think I faced future persecution. I couldn't believe it. She asked if I was going to appeal. I said, "Of course."

By this time we had heard about the coronavirus. We asked the guards, "Why don't you wear masks? You're putting us at risk." But many guards refused to wear them. They didn't give us masks, either. They never even gave us soap or hand sanitizer. The bunk beds were about three feet from each other. It was impossible for us to protect ourselves.

In April they started moving us around. Two dormitories, A and B, are apart from the others. From the yard, we could see people dressed like astronauts going into them. That's when we got really nervous. Outside, my lawyer kept asking for my parole. ICE kept denying it.

I started having a fever and difficulty breathing. On April 17, they tested me for COVID-19 and it came back positive. They moved me to Dorm A with thirty other people. If I moved, even a little, I couldn't breathe. I began vomiting and felt like I was going to drown. They hooked me up to oxygen and brought me to the hospital, drew my blood, and sent me back the same day.

My condition didn't improve. I still couldn't breathe—this time I thought I was truly going to die. Back at the hospital, the nurse told me to walk, but I fell over when I tried. They dragged me to a room where I was given oxygen again. There was a nice nurse who prayed for me and brought me strawberries, pears, and oranges. Slowly, I started getting a little better. After five days, I returned to Richwood. Instead of thirty people with COVID-19 in the dormitory, now there were fifty-five.

That's when I learned two guards at Richwood had died of COVID-19. I knew one of them, Officer Johnson. We had become friends; I told him about my life, and he told me to keep fighting. He said that sometimes he didn't want to come to work, because of how badly we were treated. They aren't supposed to do us favors, but on my birthday he gave me a chocolate.

On May 1, a guard yelled, "Raul, you have a phone call." It was Jaclyn from the Southern Poverty Law Center. "Congratulations," she said. "They're letting you go. You got parole." I didn't believe it. I called my younger sister, Margarita, who lives in Washington, and she confirmed it. Two days later, an officer said, "Grab your things, you're leaving."

Wow. Wow! I began crying. I hugged my friends. I told them, "Don't give up. Fight."

They opened the door and there was Margarita. "What do you want to eat?" she asked. I told her I didn't want to eat. "Get on the highway and drive away from here. Just get me away from here. Don't stop, don't stop, don't stop."

Note: Raul's name has been changed to protect his privacy.

Interview and editing by Gabriel Thompson. Gabriel is editor of the Voice of Witness book Chasing the Harvest: Migrant Workers in California Agriculture. *This piece was published in* Salon *on July 18, 2020.*

CLAUDINE KATETE

AGE: 26
LOCATION: Roanoke, Virginia

Claudine is a senior at Mary Baldwin University in Staunton, Virginia, finishing her final semester online. She spent most of her life in the Osire Refugee Camp in Namibia. Her family fled Rwanda in 1994 when she was two years old. She arrived in the United States in 2014 at age twenty.

When we spoke, Claudine was in her apartment in Roanoke, Virginia, where she lives with her mom and younger sister. She's grateful to spend time with her family but also worried about finding work after graduation.

I finished my courses in the social work program in the fall. We have to finish all the classes before field placement. I started my field placement with Roanoke City Department of Social Services in January. It's very practical. You practice all the things you learn and plan for in class. At the agency I worked a regular eight-hour day Monday through Thursday. Then on Fridays we had class and I caught up on assignments. In class we talked about our experiences, about assignments, and about what was going on in our field placement. We listened to our classmates' experiences and how to deal with stressful cases.

I was in my field placement for two months and then in mid-March I found out that everything was cut off. I had to stay home because of COVID-19. All the classes at Mary Baldwin went online. There were so many activities that I was still required to do for field placement, like attending advocacy community meetings. But I was unable to because those meetings were no longer happening. So I worried if I could still graduate. Luckily our program director adjusted our requirements so we could graduate and still meet our professional requirements. I continued to do my work remotely and did research to cover the hours. It's not the same though. I worked with Adult Protective Services at the agency and we did a lot of home visits. After the shutdown I didn't have direct contact with clients. I had two clients of my own that I was working with, and before I left, my cases were closed. So I had a chance to work with those clients from the beginning to the end of their cases.

Right now I'm very disappointed about graduation. I had planned a big celebration. Family and friends were coming from across the country. Even family in Rwanda that my mom reconnected with only recently, whom we haven't seen in so long, were coming to celebrate. My graduation was a reason for all of us to get together. But my plan is broken now. Mary Baldwin is planning a nice online celebration, but it won't be the same. I was going to wear the cap and gown. We won't be able to take the photographs with all our family and friends. My mother was going to see me walk across the stage. She worked so hard to get me here. My brothers can't travel from New Hampshire and even a small gathering might not be possible. I know they're all proud, but now they can't show it.

Since my field placement was going to be in Roanoke, I moved out of my dormitory and into an apartment in January, and drove to class on Fridays in Staunton—an hour's drive. My mother moved back to Roanoke from New Hampshire. She was helping my brothers there, but now we live together in Roanoke. When my sister's classes at Radford University moved online, she moved in with us, too. It's been really hard. I'm the only one working. I've been delivering newspapers for the *Roanoke Times* to pay the rent on the apartment. I work from midnight to 4 a.m., driving and taking papers from house to house. I make about $1400 a month, but the rent is more than half of that. It's really good that we're together now though. Mom has a plot at the community garden, so she grows vegetables and that helps us. We all love being with her. She takes care of us.

Before my field placement was canceled, I wasn't even sleeping. I'd come home from delivering papers and get ready to go to the agency. But now that I'm done with that agency work, I have a little more time to sleep and to apply for jobs. But I'm so worried about work and taking care of the family. I don't even know if I'm going to be able to find a job in social work because most of the places where I'm looking are closed. There are no vacancies right now. I have student loans.

I also want to go to graduate school, but I want to do that while I'm working in my profession at the same time. I don't know how I'm going to cover that. Because really, if I can't find a good scholarship, I'm going to be forced to wait for at least two years and save money for it. Hopefully, I can find a place that will hire me while I'm taking classes as well. I'm looking for clinical social work.

I want to open my own agency once I get my graduate degree, a place for social work but with high school students wanting to pursue education—like who I was when I was getting ready to go to college. I want to work with immigrants and refugees and I want to work with students directly. After high school, there are many who rush to go into the workforce. Some are pressured by their parents and I know from personal experience that some parents have cultural beliefs and traditions that keep their kids from college, especially girls. Some girls, their fathers pressure them to get married. Also, this is a new country for them and they might not have access to information. There's so much more that we can achieve if we go to college.

I wanted to be a social worker from a very young age. My mother was a single mom with four children and when we came to the camp, we were the first Rwandans. There were Ethiopians, some Sudanese, Congolese, and Burundis. There were some resources for them, but nothing for Rwandans at first. There were no scholarships for Rwandans to finish eleventh and twelfth grade. So many others got help to finish, but my mother couldn't get help to send me to finish high school. So she grew her own vegetables and saved money to send me to the Paresis Secondary School in Otjiwarongo, a small town in Namibia. I finished high school there. I had to figure it out on my own.

I really miss college because I lived on campus with friends and we'd get together at the library or the coffee shop downtown and talk about our classes and our problems. I also miss my professor, Mary Clay Thomas, the director of my program. I could go to her office and talk to her. I really cherished her support.

When I transitioned from the community college to Mary Baldwin, I stayed after class and asked her, "What do I need to know? What should I change?" I worried because for me failing was not an option.

I haven't seen my brothers in New Hampshire in a long time, but because of COVID-19 I can't see my brother who lives here in Roanoke either. His wife is pregnant and my nephew is small so we are very careful. We had to do a Zoom chat for his birthday. I haven't seen my boyfriend for two months. He lives in Maryland. We use Zoom chat a lot, too.

I hope things get back to normal. Sometimes when I think about it, you know the saying, "It is what it is." You have to live with it. When you don't have control over something, what can you do? Stressing won't help you. I learned that living in the camps.

Interview and editing by Katrina Powell. Katrina is the editor of the forthcoming Voice of Witness book Resettled: Beginning (Again) in Appalachia. *This piece was published in* Salon *on July 25, 2020.*

SOLEDAD CASTILLO

AGE: 27

LOCATION: San Francisco, California

Born in Honduras, Soledad Castillo endured sexual abuse and serious health challenges before migrating to the United States at age fourteen. After experiencing abuse in the foster care system and homelessness, she graduated from San Francisco State University and received her US citizenship. Soledad now works as a housing case manager for a nonprofit serving foster youth.

I usually work forty hours a week, but in March my hours got cut in half. I get paid hourly, a couple of dollars more than San Francisco minimum wage. It was hard because my boyfriend Alexander's hours also got cut. He works as a driver for San Francisco Paratransit and he was only working two hours a day. After my hours got cut, we started panicking. "Oh my God, how are we going to pay these bills?" Sometimes I'd go to sleep thinking about that. And then the next day: "How are we going to do this?" Thankfully, I have a friend who had some savings and she lent us some money. But can you imagine if we didn't have her? We're not prepared for this type of stuff. But how do you save when you live paycheck to paycheck?

I'm also sending money to support my family back in Honduras. My brother, my sister, and my stepfather—they all lost their jobs. I worry about them as well. I want to make sure that they have food to eat and that my mom has her medicines. Before the pandemic, I'd send money to my family once a month, but now I send money every fifteen days. I'm the only one in my family who's here in the US and has the opportunity to work and make a little bit of money. Since I came here, I always feel the pressure to help them. I have to worry about myself, but at the end of the day, they're my family and I really love them. I'm the only person that they can count on right now.

On March 17, my organization's office closed and everyone started working from home. My job is usually very in-person and one-on-one. I do home visits, help clients with their resumes, help them apply for school. The CEO of our organization sent a memo to staff to say that from now on we have to do virtual meetings with the clients. But I work with people who are disadvantaged and homeless. They don't have laptops, they sometimes don't have phones. So it's been really challenging for me to get in touch with those clients that don't have access to those services.

The first week I was working a lot. I felt so stressed because all my clients were panicking and I was panicking, too. But I was trying to control myself at the same time, to help my clients and calm them down. I had a conversation with my supervisor and we were able to get my clients computers and prepaid phones for three months. And I've been cohosting virtual classes with my supervisor, like meditation, cooking, and Zumba. I'm also emailing them resources from other organizations, like how to apply for food stamps and unemployment.

At the beginning of shelter in place, it was really tough to take care of myself. Right now it's getting better, but I still have clients calling me at 9 p.m., 11 p.m. I had to put a stop to that. I told them, "Okay, here are my office hours during the day, and you should only call me for emergencies." It was hard to set and keep those boundaries. I remember being in that situation; I was homeless in San Francisco without knowing people for three years. For me, my only family were my case managers, my social worker, and my mentors in school. So I get that. It was hard for me to say no to my clients. But I told myself that in order to help them, I have to take care of myself as well.

All of March through now, I was trying to help with my clients, but I was also going through a lot of emotional and mental pain. Back in January, I found out that I was pregnant. I'd lost a baby while pregnant the year before, so this gave me hope and I was really happy. But in February, we went to the doctor and found out that the baby was sick. We didn't know how sick. It was shocking for us because we were so excited and we didn't want to go through the same thing that we went through last year. At the time, I was hiding that from everyone and just trying to be strong.

On April 7, the doctors told us that the baby was literally dying and that they had to take the baby out because I was starting to get sick, too. That's not something you want to hear. I mean, this was my second baby that passed away. It was a really hard decision for me to make, because the baby was really sick, but his heart was still pumping and I didn't want to terminate the pregnancy.

All of this was happening while we had less money and were going through sheltering in place. I was going to a lot of different hospitals, clinics, and special offices. Alexander used all his paid time off to take me to appointments. We were finding abnormalities on every test, so out of nowhere, we'd have to go to a different hospital right away after one appointment. I was at appointments almost every week and I was always alone, talking to doctors and having them tell me that the baby was dying. Alexander couldn't come in with me, because of the coronavirus. I begged the doctor, "Please let him in. He's the father." I understood that they were trying to be safe, but at the same time, it was so hard, and I needed someone to be with me. I was heartbroken.

I was alone at the hospital the day of the surgery, from 7 a.m. to 5 p.m. The surgery lasted for three and a half hours. They said that everything went well. When I woke up, the first thing I did was call Alexander. He'd been waiting outside the whole time in the hospital parking lot.

After the surgery, I didn't want to talk to anyone. I was in so much pain and I isolated myself from people for a week. It's weird—I needed to be alone, but at the same time, I needed support. And on the days that I needed support, I wasn't able to be with anyone because of the shelter-in-place orders.

I really wanted to go see my family in Honduras, but with the virus, of course

I wasn't able to. My mom sends me WhatsApp messages every day, asking if I'm okay. Americans often talk about immigration, but we don't talk about the emotional damage that occurs when people are far away from their families. I think that not having my parents with me has affected my life a lot. I have difficulty putting myself together sometimes. Part of me is sometimes like, *Wow, what would it be like if I actually had a family with me?* And now with the pandemic, all Americans are facing similar issues. I'm not saying that it's good it's happening, but it's just a way for people to understand how hard it is to be far from your family that you love.

Besides going through the emotional impact that the death of the baby has on us, now we have to deal with the financial impact as well. The doctors did special ultrasounds on the baby's heart, lungs, and brain. Each ultrasound was like $9,000 and insurance doesn't cover those types of tests. So I'm talking to the insurance company now, trying to see if I can get any assistance or plan to pay that off.

Alexander and I are just hanging in there now and hoping for things to get better. I'm having more contact with people. I'm getting my hours back at work. I've been walking seven days a week. It's a newer thing for me. I like the smell of the trees, the smell of the flowers, the air on my face. Walking has been my therapy right now. I live in a studio apartment and it's really small. I feel that sometimes I cannot even breathe.

Note: Soledad's name was changed to protect her privacy.

Interview and editing by Ela Banerjee, community partnerships coordinator at Voice of Witness. Soledad is a narrator in the Voice of Witness book Solito, Solita: Crossing Borders with Youth Refugees from Central America. *This piece was published in* Salon *on September 6, 2020.*

BLAINE WILSON

AGE: 51
LOCATION: Tsartlip First Nation

Blaine Wilson lives in Tsartlip First Nation, in Saanich, or WSÁNEĆ, territory, about fourteen miles north of Victoria on Vancouver Island. He makes his living fishing and hunting. In Canada, Aboriginal rights, including fishing and hunting rights, are protected under the Constitution Act, and give status and non-status Indians, First Nations, Inuit, and Métis the right to participate in those activities on their ancestral lands.

Some of the following is excerpted from How We Go Home: Voices from Indigenous North America. *We spoke about how COVID-19 was impacting his life.*

My Indian name is Sluxsthet. It was my great-grandfather's name. It was my father's Indian name and is my first son's Indian name. Each family in the area has an ancestral name. It helps us. We see each other, we call each other by that name. It's like our ancestors are with us. Our name is what brings us alive, what ties us to our land because it ties us to our history here. And that's still the same today.

My dad taught me about the chainsaw, driving, hockey. He passed away when he was forty-two. He was a residential-school survivor and he took in a lot of alcohol, so probably alcohol took his life. And he was too amazing to have a short, short life. He taught me the roads, going to communities to help people having hard times, traveling to see family, to gatherings. My dad's friends and relatives, elder guys also teach me. Working together, we form crews to go get wood. A lot of people have these tools, the chainsaw, ax, and wedge, but the way we use them, nobody knows besides us.

We burn the maple and alder for smoking fish, and we use the cedars for hanging bears and we use the fir for the big fires. We make trails when we go into the forests, and it looks like a sidewalk, we've made such a good trail. Sometimes the younger people come along, so we slow down and show them, or we let them pack wood and feel what it's like to get that heavy wood up on their shoulders. They thrive.

We live seasonally, hunting and fishing; everything comes seasonally to our lives here. Like in January, we cleared the way for the new year. We physically got ready, strengthened up to go fishing in the springtime. It's a really good time of year. We've got about three boats that we like to go fishing on and once we start, we go for months, we're never home. We just head out here and do some cod fishing. We head to the mainland and do some crabbing with our cousins, and then we do the Fraser River and we fish eulachon. And we fish spring salmon. And the sockeye's really good when it happens. We get fish from Port Alberni to Nanaimo to Duncan, Merritt, or Kamloops, and anywhere in between.

When I was twenty-five, thirty, there was more salmon, and I was fishing every other day. This year I'll be lucky to go once a week. Why would there be less salmon? The globe is too warm, the water is too warm, the landslides from all the logging interrupts the river. And because everybody wanted to fish for a million. Everybody wanted to make a million bucks. So they got out there, fished like hell, and now there's no more fish. I do this for my food, for my living. And that's our connection to our ancestors. That's our medicine.

When I take my sons fishing, they listen. It really makes them happy to learn the way we do it, so they can teach their friends all the things that we do—crabbing and fishing and hunting. Once we've done the work of one task, we can go to the next. When we're catching fish, it gives us strength to go get a deer. We're not tired and weak, and we've already been busy. That's what gives us the strength. We use the same strength that we've been building to go to the next part of the calendar year. That's what we carry around.

We live on an island, so we could kind of see what was happening before it came here. We have our own border, a water border, and when COVID-19 was declared a pandemic the cruise ships were stuck in Fort Lauderdale. Their next destination was supposed to be Victoria.

I was going to start harvesting crab next week. We would be trapping April, May, June, and things start slowing down in July. My buddy's got a commercial boat that we go on. He's the skipper. He drives the boat and he relies on me to work the gear, bait the cups, and move the traps. We use a trap line, twenty-five traps.

We normally take the crab to a community shed for other people in the community to take. And then for the commercial people, we take it to a warehouse that's an hour away, in Surrey. We've watched them work there. They fix the crab up in water and air tanks so they can ship it overseas, to keep them alive for transport. The crab goes on the airplanes to Hong Kong or China. That's where the market for live crab is. The brokers, they'd put it on the airplane. They have a license to do that, going through the port. But those ports are closed down for business. No flights anywhere. So that's major. Our activities were shut down. Now we're not traveling. We don't have the tanks to keep the crabs alive. So we have to wait.

But through the years of working, I accumulated a lot of tools. And I feel like it's the old days, where we have free time to do amazing things at home. We're making stuff out of our leather. I never made moccasins before. But I have some to copy and I'm making a moccasin today. I made a bullet holder so when I go hunting in the fall the bullets will be tied to me. And I'm able to do good cleaning my own yard—and my mom's. We painted the deck. We painted the porch. Four days of painting a dock through self-isolation. And we split wood. Do good. The outlook on life is better.

If you don't get a chance to do anything, your body seizes up inside the house. The body isn't used to that restriction. We have to get out and exercise, get on the bike so we can get our legs going, so we're not hurting the knees and the back by sitting around. The physical part of the shutdown is really hard.

We had one COVID-19 death here. He was a young person. A struggling young person who didn't find the right direction. He just needed a place to go every day. He didn't have that. They don't know where he got it. For funerals we have a lot of helpers come by. That's a social change for us now. We're used to the whole community and a full week of planning for funerals. It's a really difficult time for us to go through like this. We're not used to social distancing.

We're working on holding onto everything that we have because it's left for us by our ancestors. Like a new wave of elders, we have to pass on what we have been taught. We share what we know, and we can see it on the kids if we don't share, if we haven't done our job.

The kids help us too, though. As much as we share with them, they share with us. Because we don't know technology like they do. They help us that way. We're trying online banking now because of the virus. We never had to do that. We'd always go see the banker because we knew them there. A lot of the tellers were our friends' mothers. So we didn't mind going to the bank.

We could be getting ready to go fishing. But the government asked us to not get ready. Why not? It was always keep-your-distance work. It's a lot of isolation when we go fishing anyway. We don't see anybody. So I'm hoping to get going again after all this soon.

I've put a lot of the teachings in my sons. I really hope they'll continue to make a living this way because it's been a good life. Hunting and fishing—I believe in it.

Interview and editing by Sara Sinclair. Blaine is a narrator in and Sara is the editor of the Voice of Witness book How We Go Home: Voices from Indigenous North America.

GABRIEL MÉNDEZ

AGE: 21
LOCATION: San Francisco, California

Gabriel Méndez fled Honduras at the age of fifteen, after years of experiencing sexual abuse and homophobic violence. He was granted political asylum in 2015 and is now an undergraduate student at UC Berkeley.

I'm a Spanish major. My professors in the Spanish department are pretty old, so they don't have that much Internet experience. When I started class back in January, I told a professor, "I need my computer to write and take notes." And she said, "No, we don't use computers in the Spanish department. We want students to do it on paper."

Now all of my classes are online. It's not the same learning process. In person, you stay interested. You're in a classroom and students are paying attention to the professor. You have some minor distractions, but you get whatever the professor is saying. For Spanish, you need discussions and now it's a mess. The professor won't be online or will be late, or the students will be late. Timing is hard.

Some professors are going so far as to say that they don't want to hear any other noises when you speak or see people in your background during class. Maybe the professors have their own houses and they live by themselves. Some of the students, like myself, don't have a place where we can be in the class without other people being around. If I'm at home and I want to speak, I'd have to get everyone in the house to be quiet. My whole family and I—eleven people—live in the same four-bedroom apartment. We have shared spaces and we're not able to tell each other, "Okay, move out," or "Go to the other room because I'm in class."

Professors are trying to make us do more than we're capable of doing. And that's in every class. It's three or four times harder for us students. One professor wants us to volunteer at a nonprofit with the pandemic going on. She thinks that we're at home, chilling, while actually, some of us are working, some of us are doing more than we were before.

Starting in February, I was working as a janitor for a neighborhood of apartment blocks in San Francisco. They have a lot of buildings, eleven towers—and there are about five thousand units. There are a lot of people living there. So I was still working during the pandemic because we are considered essential workers. We had to clean these spaces for thousands of residents living there and take the trash out to the compactors. If we stopped that process for even one day, it would be a mess. I worked forty to sixty hours a week.

Out of the thousands of residents at the buildings where I worked, we heard that a lot of people had COVID-19. One of them died in April. In my job, there wasn't enough protection. Because we're humans and we make mistakes, at any point, if we didn't use a glove to open a door, if we didn't wear a mask, or we didn't do something to protect ourselves, we could get the virus. Janitors weren't provided with any masks or hand sanitizers. Sometimes we'd each get three to four pairs of gloves for the day. But other times, like on weekends or if you were late to a shift, you wouldn't get any gloves at all. It was on us to take the time to go to the restroom and wash our hands. But it's hard when you're cleaning because you're not in the same spot. I worked throughout the complex. I didn't have the chance to go to a restroom and wash my hands every five minutes, and I wasn't able to get enough gloves. I wish they would've had something like disinfectant for the employees to clean our clothes or our shoes or anything. Because even if we washed our hands often, our clothes may have had the virus. We were constantly at risk of being exposed.

In early April, I got very sick. I went to the hospital, I was feeling so weird. I coughed in front of some people waiting in the emergency room and they jumped away from me because they thought that I had the virus. I have asthma so I was worried about what would happen if I couldn't breathe. What would happen if I'm at home and there's not a ventilator for me? *I'm going to be the next one on the list of statistics of how many people die every day.* I got tested and the results came back negative. After a few weeks, my cough went away. I don't know what it was that I had.

The last week of April, I left my job. I left because of discrimination. The supervisors, upper management, and other employees—they used to tell me that being gay was wrong. They'd always say that I have a demon because I'm gay. They'd say some jobs weren't necessarily for me because of my sexual orientation and they were also kind of racist at the same time. I was going to get laid off anyway. They'd been saying that they didn't have enough work for us to do and that my wage was going to go down to from $16.50 per hour to $16. My aunt was working there as well and she got laid off one day after I left.

I filed for unemployment while I try to get another job. There are really bad jobs out there. On Friday, I went to see about a janitorial position. It was at a hotel, though you could tell that people were living there and not just staying for a night. It was super-nasty and dirty. Everyone was wearing masks, inside the rooms. I felt like I'd be at high risk to get COVID-19 working there, so I left. I thought, *I'd rather file for unemployment than go into this.*

My family was worried at the beginning of the pandemic. Now they're more worried than ever because there are a lot of rumors about Latino people being impacted here in Hunter's Point and in the Mission. My family members work in the kitchens at restaurants, but only two people are working right now. Everyone else lost their jobs in March, because of the pandemic. Almost all of my family members are undocumented. They can't file for unemployment. They can't receive stimulus payments. Even though I pay taxes and I have a social security number, I wasn't able to get the $1,200 stimulus payment from the government, because I'm dependent on my mom. They aren't enough resources. My whole family is dependent on two of us who were working to get the food and pay the bills. I myself was waiting for the next paycheck when this whole thing started. Then I got into debt with all my credit cards because I needed to buy food. I had some savings, but now I'm going broke.

I spend a typical day now looking for resources for other people. A lot of coworkers asked me about what rights they have. Even some residents in that building complex would come to me saying, "Okay, I went to the AT&T store," or, "I went to Pacific Gas and Electric, but the place is closed, I don't know what to do." They'd ask," Can you get me the phone number for that place?" I try to find the right phone numbers or the right contact or the right resources so that they can get some help. Sometimes, resources are gone and you have to seek out others.

I guess a lot of older people are looking to the youth because they know that we can navigate this system better. Language is a barrier. There are less resources in Spanish. Even in a pandemic, we're still a minority. We don't get the resources. We get a barrier on everything—getting food, getting supplies. It's hard.

The end of the semester was a whole mess. I passed only one out of my three classes. With classes all online, my motivation went down. And the discrimination I experienced at my job had a big impact on my mental health. I have major clinical depression and all that stress built up. I had many breakdowns during this spring semester. If the pandemic hadn't happened, I feel like I would've passed all my classes.

Note: Gabriel's name was changed to protect his privacy.

Interview and editing by Ela Banerjee, community partnerships coordinator at Voice of Witness. Gabriel is a narrator in the Voice of Witness book Solito, Solita: Crossing Borders with Youth Refugees from Central America. *A revised and edited version of this piece with additional commentary by John Washington was published in the* Nation *on July 30, 2020.*

MICHAEL "ZAH" DORROUGH

AGE: 66
LOCATION: Corcoran Prison, California

Under usual circumstances, US prisons and jails are unhealthy and dangerous places to be, but they have been especially perilous during the COVID-19 pandemic. Across the country, prison systems have proven ill-equipped to protect incarcerated people from the virus. By the end of 2020, one in five people incarcerated in the US had contracted the coronavirus. California houses the country's largest prison population, and officials there have faced harsh criticism for outbreaks throughout state prisons.

Michael "Zaharibu" Dorrough has been incarcerated in California since 1985 for a murder he says he did not commit. Currently at Corcoran Prison, Zah spent nearly thirty years in solitary confinement throughout prisons in California. We communicated with Zah beginning in summer 2020 through winter 2020–21 through a prison email system to hear about his experience contracting the coronavirus behind bars.

Many of us are still experiencing symptoms of the virus. I'm still having serious problems with my breathing. Whenever I bend down to just tie my shoes, my breathing becomes very labored. When I try to exercise, my chest sounds very congested. I can hear my breathing. I have serious fatigue, some headaches, and two of my teeth just fell out.

There are a lot of guys here who are experiencing these symptoms. Many of us are concerned that if we say anything, they will simply quarantine us. We are tested every week, and the results are negative, so this is no longer about having the virus. We aren't being provided with support in our recovery.

I'm located now in the level-two yard at Corcoran Prison in California. I've been here since February 2020. I've been incarcerated in California State Prisons since 1985. So that would be thirty-five years and eight months.

The starting point in discussing the pandemic is that the health care department simply does not care about our well-being. And you can actually see what not caring about us looks like.

At the beginning, all we knew about COVID was based on the very limited information that we were receiving from local news coverage. We saw and heard of things like masks, social distancing, and people dying on the news, but none of this was part of our reality inside. I think that because we weren't given even basic tools like hand sanitizer, disinfectant, and so on, I developed this kind of false sense of security. This was enhanced by what we were telling each other every day, which was that the virus can only be brought inside by staff!

On some level, I did think that it was highly unlikely that those of us in prison would be impacted by this in a major way, because the only way that could happen was if people coming into the prison were not concerned with their own health. People would have to be extremely reckless for that to happen. There were only a handful of positive tests at the prison for a while. Most of the positive results were at Corcoran. As we learned more, we tried to make sure we had the materials that we needed to take care of ourselves. As time went on and we started to be impacted by it, I became a bit more concerned. We were starting to get a lot more materials sent in from the street, and that helped, but I had this feeling that we were going to go through a major outbreak at some point. I was basing this on what had happened at San Quentin and Chino, two California prisons that had seen huge numbers of COVID cases early on.

At Corcoran, it started in early summer with a free staff person in the kitchen being infected and the evening kitchen workers being quarantined. But the building itself was not placed on quarantine status. After that was over we were tested, but there were no reported positive results. We were quarantined a few weeks later, but only for seven days, not the required fourteen days. We were again tested, I think in July, and this time there was an explosion of positive results. Over a period of days, the people who had tested positive were called out and told that they would be moving to the "C" yard to be quarantined. My name was called that week.

There were at least thirty to forty people who went to the C yard at the time that I went to quarantine, but not everyone had tested positive. There were several people who were quarantined with us who had not tested positive. They should not have been there. Or at least not in quarantine with us.

When we got to the quarantine building, it was obvious that there was no plan in place. Except on one occasion, we were not given any cleaning materials, no clean bedding or clothing. And we were told that we would have to be double celled. It seemed that our being moved was just to give the impression that something was being done. We were given the same food as the rest of the prison gets.

There was no communication even among staff. I experienced many symptoms, like severe fatigue and muscle pain, headaches, a total loss of appetite, constant coughing, and congestion in my chest. My legs felt as though they each weighed a hundred pounds, and they burned constantly, especially my thighs. We had our vitals taken twice a day, and I was asked if I was experiencing any symptoms. I'd let medical know that I was experiencing symptoms and what those symptoms were, but nothing at all was done.

All I really did was sleep. I had absolutely no energy. I felt pretty helpless. Mostly because I didn't know how to make myself feel better. And because of the isolation, I started to feel all alone. Isolation just does you like that.

I wasn't concerned with dying though. I was actually thinking that I and others have been fighting too hard and for too long to go out from a virus. I won't die that way. I tried to just concentrate on taking care of myself as best as possible. We didn't have a lot of help. Staff didn't know what to do. And they were doing what they were told. And medical didn't seem to know what they were doing, or they didn't care. They were just going through the motions. Medical staff showed a total disregard for our well-being. I'd ask for something for the headaches—

Tylenol, ibuprofen, anything. But medical would tell me to get it from the previous shift. But when I would ask that shift, they would tell me that I must get it from the next shift! And this went on every day that we were housed in quarantine for the three weeks that we were there.

I was fortunate that I had this tablet and I was able to communicate with people outside. They provided me with some valuable information and support that made it possible for me to take better care of myself. You really are on your own where it involves medical issues in prison. We'd all have conversations with each other about it, and everyone felt the same way. Medical just did not care.

For the most part, all you heard over in the quarantine building from the guys was what amounted to concerns that flowed from just not knowing anything. We weren't being provided with any information at all. We didn't even know how long we might be in quarantine. On one occasion when we did have a chance to speak to staff, they really didn't have any answers because they were not provided with any information.

I had my moments when I was upset at the hypocrisy of some of the medical staff. I said to one of them, "I could never get away with acting so recklessly." If I refused to take the test, I would be given a rules violation report and kept in quarantine. But we cannot even get answers to basic questions. When we ask a question, we are ignored. We are told to "put in a sick call slip." And when we did that, we didn't get any reply. In a way I had no reason to be upset. Many of them don't care, and they were just staying true to that.

I'm not really sure what to say to people about who we are and what we are experiencing in prison. We are people. We are part of the human family. We have gone through many of the same experiences that others out there have, and continue to go through, specifically as it relates to the virus. The only meaningful difference is that many of us in here aren't getting the health care we need. And we hope that people out there have access to the kind of quality health care that inspires people to be confident that those who are responsible for their care really do care. Regardless of who they are.

Interview and editing by Mateo Hoke. Zah is a narrator in and Mateo is a coeditor of the Voice of Witness book Six by Ten: Stories from Solitary. *This piece was published in* Prism *on February 17, 2021.*

EMMANUEL RODRÍGUEZ

AGE: 28
LOCATION: Mayagüez, Puerto Rico

Emmanuel Rodríguez lives and works in a municipality on the west coast of Puerto Rico with a population of around 70,000. He lives with his wife, their two sons, his eight-year-old nephew, and father-in-law. The family shares a one-story, three-bedroom house. Darlyn works part-time as a nurse and also makes jewelry, but Emmanuel is the primary provider for his family. Emmanuel has worked as a dental assistant for seven years. He gets paid $8 an hour. When we spoke to Emmanuel, Puerto Rico had been on lockdown due to COVID-19 since March 15. All businesses were closed except for those providing essential services such as grocery stores, pharmacies, and gas stations.

There was no income coming in. I was really worried about what was going to happen. I had to pay bills and make car payments. At that time, no one was giving breaks for payments yet. Darlyn and I don't have medical insurance. I don't get coverage with my job. The government covers the kids, but my wife and I aren't eligible for Medicaid. We used to have it, but they took it away two months ago. If you exceed the limit for income, even by a dollar, they remove you. So now we have to pay for our own medications. And God help us if we have to be in the hospital, because I'd have to pay for it in cash and we just don't have it.

A regular day before COVID-19, when both Darlyn and I were working, we were like a tag team. She'd work from ten at night until six in the morning. I'd pick her up. The baby would still be asleep, but I'd have the older boys ready for school. It's rare for my father-in-law to be awake that early, so I'd leave breakfast ready for him. Then Darlyn could rest up.

I'd get to the dentist's office by 7:30 a.m. Usually I'm supposed to leave the office by 5 p.m., but sometimes it's 6:30 or even 7. That's pretty late for me. So I come home, shower, eat, and help a bit if there's anything to be done around the house. Then I just go to bed.

I keep myself on the move. At home, I do chores: washing clothes, mopping, taking out trash. I don't like anything to be dirty or out of place. I like to cook as well. Now with the lockdown, I'm basically full time at the house, and my days are pretty much cleaning and cooking. For breakfast I make eggs. My oldest son loves hot dogs and my nephew likes sausages, so I do that, too. For lunch, they love Chef Boyardee spaghetti. They've tried homemade spaghetti, but they don't like it as much. For dinner, I cook rice with beans and ham or sausages. I love fried meat! These days, I'm always in the kitchen.

Darlyn sits at the table and works with the older kids who have all their schoolwork. They get breaks when they can relax and go out in the backyard with the dogs. Other than that, we have to get groceries from stores. The lines are pretty long. We haven't been going to Sam's Club because the lines there are three or four blocks long.

I wish this whole thing would go away. I first heard about COVID-19 on the news, but I didn't really pay attention to it since it seemed far away. Around the beginning of March, my boss told us that someone in the medical center here in Mayagüez might have COVID-19 and that we should start taking more protective measures.[1] We already wear masks and gloves, but we started doubling them. We started seeing on the news that more cases were confirmed. We closed the dentist office on March 10.

At first, Darlyn was still working a couple days a week, so that really helped. But around March 20 the nursing home that she works for let her go. They knew that she had kids and they didn't want to expose her.

I knew that I'd have to go to the Departamento to ask for help and go through the same long process as when Hurricane María hit the island in 2017 and I was out

---

1. On March 13, the governor of Puerto Rico announced the first three confirmed cases of coronavirus on the island.

of work for months.[2] On March 16, I filled out the forms online. Their employees weren't working in the office and they closed down the whole building. At first I filled out the forms as if my loss of work was a temporary thing. I didn't know we'd be closed so long. I thought, *We're going to open again pretty soon hopefully.* But when I contacted one of the Departmento workers, they said, "Since the whole office is closed, you have to fill it out as if you lost the job." I filled the form out again.

I was waiting for money to come in, and it'd been three or four weeks, and I was really desperate, especially having three kids at home. There was a time when the baby didn't have diapers or baby wipes. We did have food stamps and that little bit of money from that program in cash, but it's not that much help.[3] We used it to buy Clorox. I was thinking, *Maybe I should ask my boss for some vacation pay I had.* If that didn't work 'd need to find someone who could lend me some money.

Darlyn was sad and disappointed because she'd been let go from her job and couldn't help me. She said, "I don't want you to keep paying the bills by yourself. I want to help." We always comfort each other and try to look on the bright side. We said, "We can get through this. We can try to find small jobs running errands, or our brothers and sisters in church or maybe family members can help us out." Darlyn makes jewelry and sells it online. She gets $10 or $20 a piece, and right now people are buying like crazy. She can make around $90 a week. So, that helped us a lot.

---

2. "Departamento" is short for Departamento del Trabajo y Recursos Humanos, which is the Puerto Rico Department of Labor and Human Resources.

3. The former US Food Stamp program is currently called Supplemental Nutrition Assistance Program (SNAP), but people often still refer to the assistance as "food stamps" or "los cupones." Puerto Rico was part of the Food Stamp program until 1982 when it was replaced with the Nutrition Assistance Program (NAP), or Programa de Asistencia Nutricional in Spanish. When NAP was created, funding was substantially cut and funding limits were imposed, so participants in NAP do not receive the same benefits as those in SNAP. A small portion of NAP benefits can be taken out in cash.

We finally got our first unemployment check on April 27, six weeks after I'd applied for help. We get $198 every two weeks. We also got the federal money that everybody is getting. That money came to Puerto Rico around May 2, but there are still thousands who haven't received these benefits and are waiting for help. Last week, I was that person. I didn't have anything at all.

Getting money was such a relief. But things are still difficult. I'm really afraid of another big earthquake.[4] It's also hard not being able to see family. I have a sister and niece who live in Rincón, a town not far from here. Before the lockdown, on weekends, the whole family would meet up there. We'd do a lunch or dinner and share food. Here, in Mayagüez, I have a brother from my dad's side, and we'd go to his house and watch wrestling or movies. My brother-in-law has a horse. The kids like to ride the horse a lot, so they miss that.

What I miss most is work. It keeps me sane. I like being active. I love talking with patients. My biggest worry about this whole thing was that I'd lose my job, but Dr. Deliz wants to keep his staff intact. We're talking about opening up again. Dr. Deliz has bought covers for the chairs in the waiting room, disposable gowns, and more gloves. There's going to be a plexiglass shield around the desk where the secretaries sit. He put in some special ultraviolet lights to kill germs. He's also thinking about certain things he wants to do, like checking that patients have no fever before they come in, limiting how many patients he'll be able to see in a day. It'll be fewer than before, so we probably won't work the same full-time hours as we used to. I'm worried about the economy and all the businesses that haven't been able to open yet, like our office. I worry about coming back. It's still all very uncertain.

Note: Emmanuel returned to work near the beginning of June. But almost five months

4. Starting December 28, 2019, Puerto Rico was hit by earthquakes, which was still occurring when we spoke to Emmanuel in May 2020.

after reopening, the dentist's office had to reduce its staff due to the impact of COVID-19 on business. Emmanuel was laid off on October 12, 2020. He sent out résumés that same week, and a week later he was hired full time by another dentist in Mayagüez.

Interview and editing by Marci Denesiuk. Emmanuel is a narrator in and Marci is a coeditor of the forthcoming Voice of Witness book Mi María: Surviving the Storm. *This piece was published in* Prism *on November 30, 2020.*

NINA GONZALEZ

AGE: 42
LOCATION: San Mateo, California

Nina Gonzalez immigrated to the United States from Guatemala in 1997 and lives in the San Francisco Bay Area with her husband and teenage son. She owns a cleaning business that employs ten other immigrant women, but the pandemic has severely impacted the flow of available work.

The reason I came to the United States was to save my life. When I was six years old, my father started sexually and physically abusing me. Eventually he came to the United States and then something happened that got him deported. I was eighteen at that time and when he came back home, I said, "No, you're not going to keep abusing me." One night he almost killed me and I ran out of my house.

I had a cousin who was living in San Francisco and she said, "If you want, you can borrow money and come to where I am." And I was thinking San Francisco was another part of Mexico. When I made it to San Francisco at nineteen, that's when I realized the United States is another country. Two years ago I was able to get asylum. It was life-changing because for many, many years I lived in the shadows and now I feel a little bit more comfortable. I have a social security number, I have a driver's license. I don't have to fear anything.

I started my cleaning business in 2008 and now I have ten girls who help me on a regular basis, Monday through Friday. We used to be very busy. We'd work from 8:00 a.m. to 4:30 p.m., but when COVID-19 hit in the first week of March most of my clients canceled the service and said they would reach out when the shelter-in-place order was lifted. A lot of clients sent me links and said, "Oh, you can apply for a loan and continue paying your employees," but they don't understand the situation.

Most of the women I employ don't really speak Spanish. It's really hard for them to communicate, because their first language is either Mam or some other Mayan dialect. They are all undocumented. I have to pay them cash and this is their main source of income. Most people who have a social security number can apply for unemployment. But the women who work for me, the most they can get is help with food from nonprofit organizations. We tried seeking help for rent for some of them with a local aid organization, and we were all denied. The women are really scared of being evicted. Most of these women have two or three kids. I feel the burden, because I feel that they are under my wing. It's really just heartbreaking, because as a human being, you want to do as much as you can. Each week I'm trying to see what I can do to help them a little bit, but it's really not much.

A lot of people were canceling having us come clean, but on March 6 I had to stop everything. I have about twenty clients total and they live all over the place, from San Francisco to Redwood City. There are good people out there, but there are also a lot of very selfish people. I've found that not a lot of people appreciate what we do. I have clients who said, "We'll reach out to you when the shelter in place is lifted." I sent them text messages saying, "I'm thinking about you. I hope you and your family are okay." They didn't even respond. They see cleaning as something that isn't important. They just don't care. We do things that nobody else wants to do. We deep clean the bathrooms, the toilet bowls, and the floors. We deep clean the kitchen, the countertops. We vacuum, we dust, we wipe all of the surfaces, we disinfect. They see it like it's nothing, but I think we are an essential business because we keep things clean. We work in people's homes for years and we care about their families. And then for us to be treated like this—it's kind of sad.

All the women who work for me are from Guatemala. I'm from Guatemala and I never intended to hire just from there, but I noticed that these women are really hard-working and they really love what they do. They're very smart and they're pretty fast learners. They're not friends at first, but then once they get to know each other, they become close. They text or call each other. Even if they don't know how to communicate because they speak different dialects, they figure it out. When we're all working together, they have a big smile on their faces because they see each other.

It makes me very happy that I can provide jobs for them. I also teach them Spanish and I encourage them to learn and not to be shy. Some of the women lived in very remote areas in Guatemala. When I came to the United States, I didn't have any support. I didn't have anybody telling me, "You can go to school, you can do things differently." I wish it had happened. And now I'm trying to teach them that they can do more and achieve more in their life. They cannot live in fear.

I've been hired to clean two empty houses during this time. And it broke my heart when I saw these women who work for me. They've lost their smiles. It seems like they have no hope. I remember us laughing together in the car, talking about their kids, and now everything is so quiet. Nobody talks about anything.

My own family is doing okay. We stay home a lot. My husband works for a paper shredding and recycling company, but he isn't working now because of the pandemic. The cost of living in this area, it doesn't make any sense sometimes. It's really difficult. Every dollar that we make, I make sure that I pay the girls and then everything else goes to our rent, and then food. A lot of things at this moment we cannot keep paying. We cannot pay for cable; we cut it off. We take shorter showers. We're trying to use less water, less power, all those things. We're in survival mode right now.

My business means a lot to me. I do it because I love it. I love to help others. And I can support my family through this. You know, somebody working for a tech company, they take it really seriously. I take my job seriously, too. These last few weeks, it was really worrying because I feel that all these families are depending on me and there's not much I can do. I lost my appetite. I wasn't able to sleep. All this time, you know, you just keep thinking and thinking and thinking. I felt like I was going to go crazy.

On May 18, we got good news. San Mateo County entered Stage 2 for the coronavirus, so we were authorized to go back to work. We still have to wear masks and gloves and only two people at a time can go inside each home, but at least we're doing something. So for this week I have five houses, which is great. I'm just hoping that, day by day we get more clients and then we start working a little more. If some of my clients keep losing their jobs or something else happens, then we're going to be in big trouble.

The business may not close completely, but eventually I will have to let go of more people. And I really don't want to do that. I had to let go of the two girls who started working for me most recently, and it was really, really hard. As much as I wanted to keep them, there's really not much I can do. And you know, I had to be honest with them because I cannot lie and say, "Oh, you'll be back." And then the days go by and nothing is happening. I told them that if they're going to stay in the area and if things get better, I'm happy to hire them back. But it's really hard to say what's going to happen.

Note: Nina's name was changed to protect the privacy of her employees.

Interview and editing by Ela Banerjee, community partnership coordinator at Voice of Witness. This piece was published in Salon *on September 7, 2020.*

HUNTER R.

AGE: 30
LOCATION: Albuquerque, New Mexico

Hunter was born and raised in Santa Fe, New Mexico, and has lived in Albuquerque for the past twelve years. She was working four jobs prior to the COVID-19 pandemic, and each job has been impacted differently as a result of the quarantine. The most immediate shift was losing her most lucrative job dancing at a strip club two nights a week. She maintains her job as an educator and seller at a sexuality resource shop although she no longer meets customers in the store or in the classroom because all sales and classes now take place online. While her third job as a phone sex operator continues, she is actively seeking to increase what had been a small fourth revenue stream from her internet porn.

I started noticing my own anxiety about coronavirus in January. It was occupying more and more of my brain space. I was doing a lot of, *Oh, you're just overreacting—* that kind of self-talk. Toward the end of February, I was like, *No, you're not.* That's when I started to trust my instinct a little bit more, especially because a lot of the work I do is very high contact.

Before the pandemic, I had four-ish jobs. My highest-contact jobs are that I'm a stripper and a dancer. I worked Friday and Saturday nights, which are the high-traffic nights. That typically means arriving around 8 to 10 p.m. and staying till around 3 a.m. and coming into very close physical contact with hundreds of people. And, people are feeling free and intoxicated so they're trying to put their mouths on you, which happens all the time. So, I'm hearing about the pandemic and I'd go into the club and immediately I'm thinking about all this contact with dancers and patrons—physical contact is just built into the industry of being a dancer.

I also work at a sex toy shop in Albuquerque. We are a health- and education-focused business, so we encourage people to come in and pick up the toys and touch them and use the lube sample and rub it around and smell it and taste it. We encourage people to sit and ask us questions because for so many people that's what helps them feel safe. I was in the store meeting with my coworkers and doing in-person events multiple times a week. I teach a lot of our classes with ten to eigthteen people in our classroom. And I'd go out to bars and do outreach. So, my sex shop job also had me coming into contact with lots of people.

Because of dancing I was able to work at the store. The store is an emotionally fulfilling job, but it doesn't fill my bank account. I could do the store job that I love for $13 an hour because dancing pays $25 to $50 an hour. So, my highest-contact, riskiest job was also the one paying most of my bills. That was a stark realization for me.

I was lucky that I was doing content creation and phone sex because I'm relying much more heavily on those now. I definitely have seen an uptick in people signing up for my OnlyFans page. OnlyFans is a subscription-based fan site similar to Patreon, but it allows adult content. I do webcam modeling and custom video orders for amateur porn. I recycle the content across multiple platforms— OnlyFans, ManyVids, APClips, and a few others.

I am non-monogamous, meaning I have multiple partners, and I have a partner that I have a house with and build a life and family with. We are raising his kids part-time. It's challenging and little bit scary to do that and not feel like a liability or a risk to my partner or our family because of how people react to the fact that I do sex work. I have an Instagram and I have to make sure the kids won't find me.

Some of my other partners live in New Mexico, some outside of New Mexico. I typically tell people my job is my primary partner. I have a sweet crew of people who support me—partners who take my pictures, give me feedback on my website, and I feel lucky that I have multiple humans that help me be me on the internet in this really fun way.

I've done Instagram Live strip shows that were really fun a couple of times. I did it with some other folks, but of course Instagram is not particularly friendly to adult content, so you have to be really careful. You can put your payment service in the comments of the Instagram Live, but you're definitely not going to be making several hundred dollars in an evening like you would at a strip club doing lap dances or dancing on the stage. I think I made $20 on Instagram Live.

Online sex work is not easy money, either. You have to build up a body of work, content, and that means you have to have access to resources. This is a big barrier to entry for a lot of people. You have to have the time to do it, a nice camera phone, a tablet, or laptop, and a really good internet connection to upload videos. You need some knowledge about how to edit videos and photos. The people who make a living out of this have those things or have someone else who does it for them. Trying to record content, and edit, post, and market it—that all takes hours.

The biggest thing is that you have to have a following. I see a lot of people saying, "Oh, we'll just move online," and it's really not that simple. You don't make an OnlyFans page and immediately get fifty subscribers. Building up a following is very challenging, and you have to dedicate a lot of time, energy, and skill to it. I've been doing OnlyFans for years, but intermittently.

Making porn videos for people to buy online is legal, but there are some downsides to it. Other adult platforms have started out working with sex workers, but when they become more mainstream, they boot sex workers off their platform. Also, sex work is looked down upon, and can limit my opportunities for housing, employment, et cetera. Not all landlords want sex workers in their apartments. I do not expect privacy in this work. It's realistic to expect it, but it's not a reality right now.

I loved giving lap dances because it's a really fun way to engage in a connection. I think of the strip club as a kind of funhouse, or a ride you go on at a carnival. You pay a token, you go in, and you know what you get in there is not real life, but it's really fun to hang out where you can be flirtatious in whatever way feels good.

I had one guy come in who was like, "I've never held somebody's hand before." And so I just sat on his lap and held his hand. That was a sweet moment where I got to connect with someone. I worry pretty extensively that people aren't getting their physical touch needs met. I think there are very real consequences of people not having that sort of touch. Of course, there's a lot of things that happen in the strip clubs—themes and behaviors —that are not positive. People have tried to bring weapons, people get into fights, people over consume substances—it's a rowdy party for five to seven hours. People trying to grab me while I'm dancing on stage or giving a lap dance. It's not my job to manage the crowd; it's my job to entertain them. The bouncers manage and where I dance, I feel very supported by the bouncers. I can't say how many times a night people try to take me home. They'll say, *What time are you done here? What are you doing afterwards?* My favorite response is, *Going the fuck to sleep.* Even taking a Lyft to or from the club is very risky. The driver starts waggling eyebrows at me.

I feel very fortunate that I still have work, and that I'm able to work from home. I definitely miss being able to go out and hug people. I'm a very physical touch-oriented person when I've established that that's okay to do within certain contexts. I had a friend drop off some masks to my house the other day and I was like, "Hi, I can't hug you. I miss hugging people."

I just want people to pay attention and take the pandemic seriously. I want people to think it's a big deal. I'm finding that going out of the house is becoming more and more challenging because of the anxiety and seeing how other people are acting in the world. I see people gathering in groups and not wearing masks. I see them making fun of people who are concerned about the virus and then not adhering to social distancing. I've never done well with having things around my neck and face so wearing masks is hard. And I still do it.

Interview and editing by Andrea Quijada. Andrea is a coeditor of the Voice of Witness project in incubation Living in the Digital Welfare State. This piece was published in Salon *on August 29, 2020.*

ANASTASIA BRAVO

AGE: 42
LOCATION: Bronx, New York

Anastasia is originally from Ayutla, a small town in Puebla, Mexico, and has lived in Mott Haven, a bustling neighborhood in the South Bronx, since 1995. A single mom of two teenagers, she was working as a housecleaner, mostly in homes in downtown Manhattan, before the COVID-19 outbreak brought her work to an abrupt halt. We talked in May to hear about how the pandemic has affected her and her family.

I'm Anastasia. I live with my two children. My son is going to be nineteen years old. He's graduating high school. My daughter is going to be seventeen years old. She's in the eleventh grade. Both kids are very good students, really good kids.

I'm from Mexico. We live in the Bronx, in an apartment building. In my neighborhood, there are many Mexican, many Central American, immigrants who don't have documents. There are millions of us who contribute to this country without having any status here. But we work extremely hard. We do any kind of work we can find. We clean homes, we babysit, we work in restaurants, in delis. We do any work we're able to do because we don't want to be a burden. We want to contribute to this country. I want people to know that we're human beings, that we might have very little, but we contribute to the well-being of this country.

Before the COVID-19 pandemic, my normal day was to go work on the subway. I was cleaning homes downtown. At the end of the day, I'd come back, be with my children, help them do homework, prepare dinner, go to sleep, and get ready for the next day. I worked for different people each day, in total, five homes. And I'd go to each house every two weeks. I also worked cleaning a small independent school in East Harlem on Wednesdays and Saturdays.

I started hearing about coronavirus in early March. Then people started to die, and the school my kids go to closed. And that's when I stopped working. It was March 13. The people I was working for, they told me, "The virus has become very dangerous." They had to protect their families, and I had to protect mine. At the beginning, they told me that it would only be for two weeks, that the virus was spreading. But then, as you know, the time just went on. With two of my employers, I haven't had any contact. The other three have expressed concern about what's happening to my family. They asked, "How can we help?" They told me not to worry, that they would help me during those two weeks. They've continued to support me and I'm very grateful.

I haven't been able to get everything we need, but I've been able to get the basics. I've managed to keep a roof over my head and my children's heads, and I've been able to provide them and myself with food. During a typical day now, I'm at home with my kids. We cook together. In the morning, we'll either have a sandwich or eggs with toast, you know, a light meal. And then later on in the afternoon, we make a lunch that's more of a meal, a real meal. We do chores together at home. They do their homework too because they have school also. So I've been spending more time with them and that's the one nice aspect of what's been happening. I truly cherish that I'm able to spend full days with my kids. I'm very grateful that the three of us are in good health, that we are taking care of each other, staying here at home together.

But I'm concerned about what's going to happen, when I'll be able to go back to work. I might be able to go back to work cleaning the homes of those three people who've been helping me, but I haven't heard anything from the other two. And I don't know when or if the school that I was cleaning will open again. So I really don't know.

We have a friend of the family who died. He was sick for three weeks in the hospital. That had a tremendous impact on us, it really made us realize how serious this was, how dangerous this virus was. That's when we decided to stay at home and only go out to the store to buy the necessities. And to be protected with everything we could get a hold of—face masks, gloves, whatever else.

In the neighborhood, the silence is now so noticeable. The streets are empty. I go to the window along with some of my neighbors to applaud the medical workers at seven o'clock each evening. I shake my maracas to thank all those people who've been working so hard to keep people alive. Only five or six of my neighbors are willing to go to their windows. The fact that so few people are willing even to risk that means that there has really been an enormous change.

The neighbors, we used to talk with each other. Now we cannot do that. Before I'd walk on the street, find someone I know, and hug and chat with them. We'd laugh with each other, shake hands with each other. Now no hugs. No handshaking. Not even a minimum of conversation. Everyone is just rushing home. Everything has become about disinfecting, disinfecting yourself.

I miss my routine, going out to work. I miss the feeling of being able to do something for myself, for my children, to be able to support them. I miss meeting my neighbors and friends on the train and talking to them about their children, my children, whether they're leaving work early or not. I miss the contact, the day-to-day conversation. It's like I'm all alone. That I have to be alone. The door has to stay closed. I'm afraid.

Sometimes I wish my extended family was nearby. I really feel the need to see my mother because all of this. It's so terrible. I'm so afraid. I need a hug, my mother's hug. But she's far away. She's in Mexico and it's been many years since I last saw her. Thankfully, our town is far away from the city so she's pretty safe. It's not that I'm pessimistic, but I keep thinking that if I end up dying of this, I'm going to die without having gotten a hug from my mother.

I feel we have no voice, undocumented people. I didn't come here to take anything away from anybody else. We just want to be able to live. I want to have the opportunity to be accepted here, to have status. People want us to go back to our country, but they don't understand that it's very difficult for us to just take our stuff and go back. Our children grew up here, they speak this language here. We have roots here now. They don't even know the family that I left behind. It's very difficult. I can't just bring them back to an unknown place.

We work and we pay taxes based on the money that we earn. But we don't receive any economic aid from the government. We're not able to qualify for anything. I need economic aid from the government during this time. Many people like myself depend on charity, on the goodness of people. But basically we're at their mercy— it's the only way in which we've been able to survive.

Note: Anastasia's name was changed to protect her privacy.

Interview and editing by Dao X. Tran, managing editor at Voice of Witness. Translation provided by Selma Marks. This piece was published in Salon *on August 17, 2020.*

Illustration by Hannah Lee

YUSUFU MOSLEY

AGE: 68
LOCATION: Bronzeville, Chicago

Yusufu Mosley was born in Columbia, Mississippi. When he was eight years old, his family moved north, first to Detroit and soon thereafter to Chicago. Incarcerated as a young man, Mosley spent twenty-two years in prison. Since his release, he has become an activist-educator on the South Side. Inspired by the example of Ella Baker, Mosley facilitates peace circles, organizes for the rights of incarcerated people, and advocates for food security in underserved Black and Brown neighborhoods. He currently works as simba wasai *(village elder) with a local community organization. He lives in Judge Slater Apartments, public housing for seniors. In May 2020, he spoke with Audrey Petty about how COVID-19 has affected his life.*

I live on the South Side of Chicago, on 43rd and Cottage Grove, in a high rise. When I get tired of the apartment, we have a park area that you can go sit in and watch what's going on in the streets. But now I go sit and the streets are almost empty.

I'm in here by myself right now except for my books and papers, and I don't feel isolated. I can go down the hall and see how other people are doing and if they need anything. Most of them don't have family members who come to see them or are concerned about them. Some of them are going in their eighties. And when they get to know you—I'm like an adopted son, even though I'm sixty-eight years old. They need that kind of caring where people will look out for them and not demand something back. You feel a lot of anxiety coming from people.

I'm not a TV fan. I watch the news and have to turn it off because that's all they talk about: the pandemic. And then it seems—even if they'd probably deny it—they're focused on what whites are experiencing and how now they're protesting to open back up so they can get on with the business of making money even though at the same time they're showing a Black factory of meat cutters—Black and Brown—cutting meat. And they ain't got no masks, they ain't got no protection, and they've said nobody's brought that to them. And Trump is encouraging them to work as if their lives don't matter. Recently he and his vice president were in the middle of a room with everyone else wearing face masks— and they're the only two that don't have them. That's symbolic to me. Like they're saying, "See, I told you we're better than the rest of the world. We don't have to wear masks."

Before the pandemic, how my average day would look depended on what day it was. Three days of the week, I'd go to the library. Take notes, make copies, and then I usually come back home. I have a lot of things I'm researching at one time. One of the things that has always concerned me is culture: what is it? So I go back to where Black culture begins and that's in Africa. I'm talking about culture as ways of life, not just dance, song, and stuff like that. I want to know what the values were before outsiders came in and imposed their values and their systems of operation. I'm focused more on how African people saw themselves, and how they responded to how they saw themselves. Maybe I try to share some of those values and understandings from a particular history and culture that has really been suppressed. One of the reasons I do it so intensely is because it's fragmented.

Most recently I work with groups who call themselves Pan-Africanists. Some call themselves cultural nationalists. The work I do, it's mostly looking for alternatives to the so-called American way of life: individualistic, rugged individualism, and dogmatic, seeking profits. So we're looking for an alternative to that kind of living.

I love to read. And one of the things this situation has forced me to do is systematize my reading. As I'm talking to you, I'm looking at three books: one on the Haitian Revolution, one on Angola in the 17th century, and one on Nicaragua and the founder of the Sandinista front, Carlos Fonseca. Not being able to go to the library has been very disappointing, but I've got books. I go back and read the books that I've read already and often think of something new.

My challenges really didn't begin with this pandemic. I was in prison for 22 years, so I'm used to lockdowns and that kind of stuff, where you can't go nowhere even if you want to. The only problem was that I had a cellmate then. It's hard to explain. You don't want to be in the cell by yourself, but you also want to be in the cell by yourself because self-reflection is part of that experience. You're exploring "am I really who I am" type of thinking. But you're in a cell big enough to be a closet. And my cellmate: he didn't read, he didn't write, he didn't even write home even when he got a letter. Every time I got a letter, I wrote. In fact, I used to buy embossed envelopes. We called them write-outs. I used to buy a box of write-outs—what about, a hundred or so— so I could keep up with people. Prison was just a physical confinement. I didn't want to be there mentally. A cellmate—they can be a friend or just be somebody who occupies a space on the top bunk.

Here I don't have anybody else in the apartment except myself, so the challenge for me is to maintain the same spirit I had in prison. The longest I ever stayed on prison lockdowns was about fifteen months, where you couldn't leave the cell and they wouldn't allow any visits. The task for me is to have the mentality I had then. *I'm gonna get through it. It will pass. And be careful.*

In prison, you have to watch out for yourself, especially if you're not running with one of the gangs. You're almost always looking over your shoulder or keeping your ears open so you hear things that the guards wouldn't hear, like when they're planning on having a big fight or something like that. I've taken that experience to be watchful of what I do and who I associate with, but also you have to look out for danger when danger's coming even if nobody else sees it. And I don't have clairvoyance in that area, I just know to look out. You know, like this thing here: I'm still confused about this virus. Where it comes from and how it attacks you—all of that. So rather than sit around and argue where it came from with the people I know, I just say, "What are we gonna do about it?" And it boils down to, "What are you doing to do about it, Yusufu?"

Since the quarantine started, I've lost ten people who were very close to me in one way or another, and I won't be able to say goodbye because of the restrictions on funerals. And one person, I talked to two days before her husband called to tell me she had died. She had just gotten out of the hospital for having a heart attack, and I was chiding her because nobody told me. Her children didn't tell me and, of course, her ex-husband didn't tell me. It still breaks my heart now to even talk about it because we were good friends. The funeral is on the 8th, but it will be limited to ten people and no hugs, no handshakes will be permitted. And now you have to wear a face mask and the one I have, I can't even breathe when I got it on, so I'd have to take it down every now and then. But I ain't going nowhere, so I haven't had it on.

I don't know if all ten people died directly because of COVID, but some of the people I knew, they had other problems, too. So it's related to the lack of health care. There's been the revelation that Blacks and Latinos and Native Americans are the primary ones assaulted by this disease. My baby sister, who lives in Arizona, is very tight with the Navajo community there. And she's telling me that they're really suffering on the reservation. They don't have running water in some places. I know that's hard. Those kinds of things distress me.

But in the midst of those ten deaths, there was a sign of hope. I had a grand-niece born, two weeks into the thing, and my niece has sent pictures. I think there are about twelve pictures where she's looking into the camera and she's smiling. They tell me it's deliberate, that she does that all the time. When she wakes up, she don't cry like regular babies. S,he starts talking. They're thinking of changing her name to a feminine version of my name because she always talks and I'm always talking. I don't know if there's a feminine version of Yusufu, but they call her Imani now, which is Swahili. It means faith.

Interview and editing by Audrey Petty. Yusufu is a narrator in and Audrey is the editor of the Voice of Witness book High Rise Stories: Voices from Chicago Public Housing. *This piece was published in* Salon *on August 23, 2020.*

MOHAMMED "MIKE" ALI

AGE: 42
LOCATION: Hayward, California

Mohammed "Mike" Ali did not know he was not a US citizen until he was in his twenties. Born in Fiji, Mohammed moved with his family to the San Francisco Bay Area as a child, where he turned to gang life in the 1990s in an attempt to protect himself and his friends from bullying they experienced as immigrants. He spent much of his teens and twenties in juvenile hall, jail, and prison before being sent to immigration detention to await deportation at age twenty-four.

He spent much of the next four years in solitary confinement while fighting to stay in the US. His case was eventually successful, and he was released from solitary confinement and incarceration. Mohammed has spent the last thirteen years working a series of janitorial and maintenance jobs while taking care of his family, including his brother's four boys. One of these boys, whom Mohammed raised for most of his life, died tragically during the interview process for this narrative, which began in May 2020. During one of the worst public health°°° crises in US history, millions of Americans have lost their employer-based health insurance, Mohammed included.

It's very expensive here in the Bay Area. You've got to have two jobs to survive. I was working two jobs before quarantine, part time. A delivery job, and doing janitorial for the parks system. In the parks I was responsible for two buildings, which had preschools. I'd have to clean the bathroom, mop, sweep, disinfect a lot of stuff, vacuum, clean the windows, take all the trash out, make sure all the supplies are refilled. So it was a busy day, but it was cool.

I used to leave home at three o'clock in the morning. I'd work janitorial until nine in the morning, come home and sleep for a couple of hours, then go back to work at two in the afternoon doing deliveries. My whole day was like sixteen hours.

When the coronavirus outbreak started here, the parks closed. As soon as California did that stay-at-home order they closed like three days later. They shut the whole park system down. They laid us off. My health insurance lapsed when I got laid off. I can't afford to buy it right now because it's expensive. I'm hoping that in August I can get back to work, but there's no guarantee. I don't have security like I did before. But what can you do? That's part of life. Nothing's guaranteed. A lot of people got laid off, but I was blessed that I had this other job and kept everything afloat.

So now I just work for Unity Couriers, driving delivery and picking up, almost forty hours a week. We pick up and deliver bags of presorted mail to the grocery stores, banks, hospitals. It's stable work because we're essential workers. I start at two in the afternoon and work till eleven at night, driving around, making deliveries. Pick up, then drive to the next one. Deliver, pick up. They give us masks, but they don't give us cleaning supplies. I use my own car.

I have a lot of downtime now because I only have one job. It's making me lazy. My body's used to working a lot. I don't have energy like I did before. I used to have a lot of energy cause I was always moving around. Now, my body's just crashing. Not being able to do anything, I'm like, *Shit, I can't sit around, I've got to be out and about.* It was out of the blue that everything shut down. No one thought this would ever happen.

The hardest part is like, what do you do when you want to go get some lunch, and stores are closed? Or they're backed up and you have to wait outside for an hour or two? Most stores are closed, except grocery stores, pharmacies, and liquor stores. A lot of doctor's offices, they're closed too now. So if you're sick or anything, you have to go to the emergency room.

I have noticed a lot of people being more religious now. And people being nicer human beings, being courteous and kind and stuff. Walking down the street, people that you would never expect to talk to you, they'll talk to you, you know? People seem more engaged with life and society.

I just go on about my day. I take precautions, you know, like wash my hands, sanitize things, and all that. I was doing that before because you know, I touch a lot of stuff. I try to take precautions because my dad's older; he's seventy-six. He's staying home, but nobody else is. I haven't really been distancing from anyone. I still go hang out with my sisters, see my nieces, nephews. But I try not to go the days I'm working just in case I might have it on my clothes, you know? Or I take them off, put on clean clothes, shower, and then go visit.

There's six of us living in a three bedroom. It's me, my wife, my dad, and three kids. I raised my brother's kids. They're seventeen, nineteen, twenty, and twenty-one. The three youngest live with me. We all chip in for rent. One worked at a graphics company, but they laid him off. The youngest two work at a Jack in the Box. They still work. My wife got laid off too. She was a coordinator for the county child support department.

The good thing is we're a big family so we always stay well stocked. Our Fiji community's a little different because we came from a third world country, so we always try to have plenty of groceries. You know, if something goes wrong and the town floods, you can't go shopping. You have everything at the house to survive. Also, we'd go bulk shopping because if we buy little amounts, we'd spend more money. It's cheaper to buy large quantities and then we don't have to worry about it for a couple of months. We always have at least one or two months' worth of supplies in our house.

But honestly, I do think people need help out here. A lot of people don't have jobs and they're struggling to pay bills. And not only that, stores are marking up the prices. All the things you could get before for $1? Now they're like $5, $10. If you go to a grocery store right now, an onion that was maybe forty-nine cents a pound is like a dollar something a pound. A tub of ice cream that used to be $5 is $12.

What scares me the most is that they're saying the second wave of coronavirus infections is going to be worse when it comes in the winter. I don't think a lot of places will be open. Maybe they'll close the whole country down the second time.

You know? I'm going to find more hand sanitizer and a generator and other stuff, too. I'm going to be prepared.

Interview and editing by Mateo Hoke. Mohammed is a narrator in and Mateo is a coeditor of the Voice of Witness book Six by Ten: Stories from Solitary.

Illustration by Jose Cruz

OSCAR RAMOS

AGE: 47
LOCATION: Salinas, California

Oscar Ramos teaches second grade in Salinas, which is the capital of the Salinas Valley and known as the "salad bowl of the world." The majority of his students are the children of farmworkers, who continue to work during the pandemic. Oscar grew up in a labor camp near Salinas and worked in the fields until the eighth grade.

This is my twenty-fourth year teaching and I've never experienced anything like this. Right before coronavirus, our school district was at the end of our second trimester. We were assessing the students in reading, writing, math. We were getting ready for parent conferences and report cards. But in early March, schools shut down and we weren't able to do any of that.

I'd been watching the news on a daily basis and kind of monitoring the situation. A lot of our kids watch the Spanish-language news with their parents. It would scare them, so they'd come into class in the morning and ask if I knew what the coronavirus was and if I knew that people were getting sick. I would tell them that, yes, I am watching the news, but I would steer them away from that conversation momentarily. I didn't want to shut them completely down because that's not healthy. I did give them opportunities throughout the day here and there to ask a question, but I didn't want that to be the main conversation of the day.

I thought that school would be shut down at some point, but I didn't know it was going to be so soon. The last day I saw my students in person was March 12. I was about to go to LA for a conference. On Thursday afternoon, I told them to behave and to help the substitute do other work with them. And the next day, Friday, the school district said they were going to shut down until further notice. I didn't get to say goodbye.

Now we're doing what everyone else is doing—Google Hangouts, Google Meets. Our school used some funds a while ago to purchase Chromebooks and iPads. So everyone has a one-on-one device. We had to distribute all this technology to the students and it took several weeks. And then we had the problem of the internet. Did they have access to Wi-Fi? And if not, what good would it do for them to have a device if they didn't? Our district purchased hundreds of hotspots for parents so they can access Wi-Fi.

But many of our kids' parents aren't familiar with the programs we use. I teach at Sherwood Elementary School, where 98 percent of our population is Hispanic. The majority of parents are farmworkers with little to no formal education. They don't know how to troubleshoot anything on the computers. They don't know how to log in, they don't know how to get messages from teachers.

Some of the students are lucky because they have older siblings who already know how to use these programs. But those that don't have those systems of support are the ones who are struggling and are the ones that we don't hear from often, if at all. I have twenty-five students. When we first started doing Google Meet or Google Hangout, I'd get six out of twenty-five students and then later it went to eight out of twenty-five. Right now I'm at eleven out of twenty-five.

We do have a list of students we haven't been able to communicate with at all. Not once. It's not an enormous list, but there were about fifteen students out of 145 total second graders that we don't know what happened to them and their families. They never came to pick up a computer. Sherwood is a food distribution center, but they never came to pick up lunches or school supplies or anything. We've tried calling their cell phones, both the mom and the dad. If there's a home number and there's no answer, no one's heard from them. Two of those missing students are from my class. We don't know where they went. If they left, or if they're here and they're just not communicating with anyone.

For the kids who can attend the Google Hangouts, at first they're a little nervous and a little scared and there's not much talking. It's kind of like when the school year first starts, they come in and they're very shy and quiet. But after a while they feel more comfortable and they look forward to the meetings. These are second graders. They do drawings and they put them up to the computer camera. They talk about their pets. It's wonderful to hear them laugh and share stories. They miss school, their teachers, their friends. They miss running around and yelling and recess. And they miss the lessons. They miss learning new things.

I miss being in the classroom with the kids. That's twenty-five students, twenty-five different personalities, and I love every one of them. You know, you have the ones that love to share. You have those who are quiet but communicate with you in different ways, with the way they look, the way they act. They're very, very kindhearted. They care for one another. I just miss the conversations, the laughter, the questions when they say, "I didn't understand that. Can you help me?" or "Can you repeat that?" That sort of relationship building happens when you're in the same room. It's not the same through a camera and a computer. I miss the little hugs they give you in the morning and the high fives when they're going home.

Twice a week my colleagues and I meet virtually so we can collaborate and share our lesson plans. But these meetings on the computer—they are exhausting. You're sitting on a chair looking at a computer and yes, you can see your colleagues, but it's not the same as sitting in the staff lounge and having a conversation while you're having a snack. It's not the same as chatting with them after school about how their day went and what they're going to do tomorrow and what we could share for future lessons. It gives me a headache. It hurts our eyes just to meet with the students virtually, to meet with our colleagues virtually, to have a staff meeting virtually, everything. I cannot stare at the computer for that long. It's great to hear their voices and see their images, but we miss that human interaction.

I don't know what idea people have about what teachers are doing now. But we're working harder than before. We're learning new programs and we're teaching the kids how to use these new programs. We're spending more time planning than ever, more time working than if it was just a regular day and it's stressful. But we're not going to let that show when we're doing our class meetings because we want the kids to think that even though it's different, we're okay and they're going to be okay.

When you're seeing the kids and they can see you, you have to continue being yourself. You can't show that you're exhausted and that you're tired of meeting virtually. It's like a performer, right? They can be exhausted, but people paid money to go see a performer. And so whatever's going on, they have to shut it off and go out there and perform. Well, with the students, it's the same thing. If we're sad, exhausted, and not really motivated, they're going to see that. The kids do detect changes and if they're not good changes, it's going to hurt them. They're not going to feel motivated. They're going to feel like, "Well, if he's feeling that way, then what about me? So you have to continue being who you were in the classroom. You smile, you laugh, you joke. They can say, "That's my teacher. That's who I was with in the classroom."

I had to tell the kids that the next time I'm going to see them in person, they are no longer going to be my students. They are going to be in third grade. And they were shocked. Their little faces with eyes wide open like, "What? How? Why?" I had to explain that they're not going to come back this school year and that I missed them dearly. So I did promise them that when they're in third grade and they're able to go back to school, I will call them all in during their lunchtime and we will have a fun lunch and celebrate that we're all back to school and that we all get to see each other again. And they liked that idea because they didn't want it to end this way. Obviously nobody did. But they'll look forward to that and I look forward to that as well.

Interview and editing by Ela Banerjee, community partnership coordinator at Voice of Witness. Oscar is a narrator in the Voice of Witness book Chasing the Harvest: Migrant Workers in California Agriculture. *This piece was published in* Prism *on December 21, 2020.*

ACKNOWLEDGMENTS

Working on this series has felt heavy at times, grappling with the multifaceted ways in which this pandemic has distilled and made more stark already existing inequities and systemic oppression. But it has also been a balm to note the resonance the pieces had when they were initially published, anchored by VOW's "slow" oral history methodology and reliance on the community bonds we've built over years of partnerships and collaborations and continue to nurture.

Thank you to our Voice of Witness colleagues—Kathleen Brennan, Liz Duran, Colleen Hammond, Mimi Lok, Cliff Mayotte, and Erin Vong—for supporting the creation of this project and for being our warm, steadfast home base during turbulent times. Thank you also to the Voice of Witness board: Aneesha Capur, Kristine Leja, Lupe Poblano, Nicole Janisiewicz, and Niles Xi'an Lichtenstein.

We nod co-conspiratorially at Marci Denesiuk, Virginia Eubanks, Mateo Hoke, Audrey Petty, Katrina Powell, Andrea Quijada, Sara Sinclair, Gabriel Thompson (editors of past, current, and forthcoming Voice of Witness collections), and Selma Marks (for attentive and sensitive translation), who nimbly turned on recorders and opened laptops to help document a still-unfolding crisis.

Gratitude to our media partners, who helped amplify these narrators' voices in their pages online and in print: Malik Meer at the *Guardian*, Erin Keane at *Salon*, Tamar Sarai Davis and Ashton Lattimore at *Prism*, and John Washington at the *Nation*.

Finger snaps to the good people at Haymarket Books, who support and publish the VOW book series, especially Anthony Arnove, Dana Blanchard, Nisha Bolsey, Rachel Cohen, Eric Kerl, Julie Fain, and Maya Marshall.

Amber Bracken's cover image of handmade masks captured the ethos of care and beauty in relying on your community in uncertain times. Erik Freer's design savvy elevated this collection. Greg Ballenger, Jose Cruz, Hannah Lee, and Christine Shields—your dignified portraits of narrators helped us "see" them all over again.

To the narrators who took time *in the midst of a pandemic* to share publicly their experiences of living through that first year: Mohammed "Mike" Ali, Anastasia Bravo, Soledad Castillo, Michael "Zah" Dorrough, Hanima Eugene, Farida Fernandez, Nina Gonzalez, Raul Luna Gonzalez, Claudine Katete, Shearod McFarland, Gabriel Méndez, Yusufu Mosely, Hunter R., Oscar Ramos, Emmanuel Rodríguez, Roberto Valdez, Blaine Wilson, we see you and we hear you.

ABOUT THE VOICE OF WITNESS BOOK SERIES

The Voice of Witness oral history book series amplifies the voices of people directly impacted by—and fighting against—injustice. We use an ethics-driven methodology that combines journalistic integrity and a humanizing, literary approach.

VOW's work is driven by the transformative power of the story, and by a strong belief that an understanding of systemic injustice is incomplete without deep listening and learning from people with firsthand experience. Titles in the VOW Book Series include:

HOW WE GO HOME
Voices from Indigenous North America
Edited by Sara Sinclair
"A chorus of love and belonging alongside the heat of resistance." —Leanne Betamosake Simpson

SOLITO, SOLITA
Crossing Borders with Youth Refugees from Central America
Edited by Steven Mayers and Jonathan Freedman
"Intense testimonies that leave one . . . astonished at the bravery of the human spirit." —Sandra Cisnero

SAY IT FORWARD
A Guide to Social Justice Storytelling
Edited by Cliff Mayotte and Claire Kiefer
"Reminds us the process through which we document a story is as important and powerful as the story itself." —Lauren Markham

SIX BY TEN
Stories from Solitary
Edited by Mateo Hoke and Taylor Pendergrass
"Deeply moving and profoundly unsettling." —Heather Ann Thompson

CHASING THE HARVEST

Migrant Workers in California Agriculture
Edited by Gabriel Thompson
"The voices are defiant and nuanced, aware of the human complexities that
spill across bureaucratic categories and arbitrary borders." —*The Baffler*

LAVIL

Life, Love, and Death in Port-Au-Prince
Edited by Peter Orner and Evan Lyon
Foreword by Edwidge Danticat
"*Lavil* is a powerful collection of testimonies, which include tales of violence, poverty,
and instability but also joy, hustle, and the indomitable will to survive." —*Vice*

THE POWER OF THE STORY

The Voice of Witness Teacher's Guide to Oral History
Compiled and edited by Cliff Mayotte
Foreword by William Ayers and Richard Ayers
"A rich source of provocations to engage with human dramas
throughout the world." —*Rethinking Schools Magazine*

THE VOICE OF WITNESS READER

Ten Years of Amplifying Unheard Voices
Edited and with an introduction by Dave Eggers

PALESTINE SPEAKS

Narratives of Life under Occupation
Compiled and edited by Cate Malek and Mateo Hoke
"Heartrending stories." —*New York Review of Books*

INVISIBLE HANDS

Voices from the Global Economy
Compiled and edited by Corinne Goria
Foreword by Kalpona Akter
"Powerful and revealing testimony." —*Kirkus*

HIGH RISE STORIES
Voices from Chicago Public Housing
Compiled and edited by Audrey Petty
Foreword by Alex Kotlowitz
"Gripping, and nuanced and unexpectedly moving."—Roxane Gay

REFUGEE HOTEL
Photographed by Gabriele Stabile and edited by Juliet Linderman
"There is no other book like *Refugee Hotel* on your shelf." —*SF Weekly*

THROWING STONES AT THE MOON
Narratives from Colombians Displaced by Violence
Compiled and edited by Sibylla Brodzinsky and Max Schoening
Foreword by Íngrid Betancourt
"Both sad and inspiring." —*Publishers Weekly*

INSIDE THIS PLACE, NOT OF IT
Narratives from Women's Prisons
Compiled and edited by Ayelet Waldman and Robin Levi
Foreword by Michelle Alexander
"Essential reading." —Piper Kerman

PATRIOT ACTS
Narratives of Post-9/11 Injustice
Compiled and edited by Alia Malek
Foreword by Karen Korematsu
"Important and timely." —Reza Aslan

NOWHERE TO BE HOME
Narratives from Survivors of Burma's Military Regime
Compiled and edited by Maggie Lemere and Zoë West
Foreword by Mary Robinson
"Extraordinary." —Asia Society

CPSIA information can be obtained
at www.ICGtesting.com
Printed in the USA
JSHW030041240921
18957JS00005B/41